THE ENCOUNTER

DISCOVERING GOD THROUGH PRAYER

The term "Spiritual Exercises" means all of the ways of examining the conscience, meditating, contemplating, and praying aloud or in the mind, and all other spiritual activity.

Just as strolling, walking, and running constitute physical exercises, so also the Spiritual Exercises constitute all of those ways of preparing and disposing the soul to throw off of itself all disordered affections, and to seek and find the divine will in the disposition of one's own life, for the salvation of the soul.

—Saint Ignatius of Loyola,
Spiritual Exercises (1548)

It is not necessary to be Catholic or Christian, a believer or a humanist, to have an interest in the Spiritual Exercises of Ignatius of Loyola.

—Roland Barthes,
Sade, Fourier, Loyola
(1971)

THE ENCOUNTER
DISCOVERING GOD THROUGH PRAYER

Cardinal Gianfranco Ravasi

SAINT BENEDICT+PRESS
Charlotte, North Carolina

Typeset by Lapiz

Cover design by Ryan Scheife

ISBN: 978-1-61890-126-2

Published in the United States by
Saint Benedict Press, LLC
PO Box 410487
Charlotte, NC 28241
www.SaintBenedictPress.com

Printed and bound in the United States of America

CONTENTS

FOREWORD

"Within me there is a spring that is very deep. And in that spring is God. Sometimes I am able to reach it, more often it is covered with stone and sand: in that moment God is buried, so one must dig him up again." It was November 30, 1943, and in Auschwitz in a gas chamber, the twenty-nine years earthly life of a young Dutch woman, Etty Hillesum, was dissolved. A few months earlier, in her *Diary*, she had written the lines which we have cited and which can be taken freely as a symbolic representation of the Spiritual Exercises. They are like a liberation of the soul from the soil of things, from mire of sin, from sand and from triviality, from the nettles and weeds of chatter.

There are so many ways to unearth the voice of God, which may have become faint within us. We have decided to follow a privileged path for rediscovering the purity of the faith, entrusting ourselves to a classical motto: *lex orandi, lex credendi*; the guide, the norm for genuine belief is the way of prayer in all of its manifold iridescence. In fact, we have wished to add a further variation: *ars orandi, ars credendi*. Prayer is also an art, an exercise of beauty, of song, of inner liberation. It is ascesis and ascent, it is a rigorous effort, but also a gentle and free flight of the soul toward God. To use an evocative definition of the liturgy in its intimate structure proposed by the philosopher Jean Guitton, it is *numen* and *lumen*, it is mystery, transcendence, objective reality, a divine word that is unveiled in us, but it is also human contemplation, joyful adherence, a song of the lips and of the heart.

The pole star for living this experience is, then, the biblical Psalter, a dazzling representation of the dialogical aspect of Revelation. The prayers of the Psalms are, in fact, human words; and yet they bear upon themselves the seal of divine inspiration, so that God is speaking in them as well. As Dietrich Bonhoeffer, the theologian who was eliminated in the Nazi atrocities, said in his booklet on how to "pray with the Psalms, if the Bible contains a book of prayer, we must deduce that the Word of God is not that which he wants to address to us, but is also that which he wants to hear us address to him." There is good reason that the Jewish tradition divides the 150 Psalms into five books and places it beside the divine Torah as a "Torah" of prayer. The Psalms are a response of faith and love to the Torah.

Precisely because of this twofold dimension that the Psalter and prayer reveal, the journey that we will make together will also be twofold. First, however, let us pause to seek to delineate the intimate essence of prayer, a term of Latin origin that is particularly evocative because it is related to *orare*, "to pray," but also to "proclaim" (commemorative public oration): in action it is, therefore, the *os*, the "mouth," the lips that invoke and that in *adorare* can also refer to the hand brought to the mouth for a kiss given to the beloved divinity. But as will be seen, precisely because it is the mouth that sings, there also inevitably enters into action the breath, a sign of physical and interior life.

From this initial threshold our journey of prayer will follow, as has been said, two necessary movements. The first is upward: it will lead us toward the heights of transcendence, toward the mystery, the *numen* in point of fact. This is God, about whom prayer will show us various profiles that the faith is able to define in its various meanings. From there the journey is downward: the resplendent light of the face of God (cf. Nm 6:25; Ps 31:16 (RSV): "Let thy face shine on thy servant") illuminates, in fact, the manifold features of the human face. God and the human creature, theology and anthropology meet, therefore, at the crossroads of prayer; a necessary intersection, as the well-known French aviator and author of *The Little Prince*, Antoine de Saint-Exupéry (1900–1944), suggested: the men of today "lack nothing except for the golden knot that holds all things together. And then everything is lacking."

PART ONE

THE FACE OF GOD

David is our Simonides, our Pindar, our Alcaeus,
our Flaccus, our Catullus. He is the lyre that sings
Christ!

—Saint Jerome, *Epistula
LIII ad Paulinum*

CHAPTER I

BREATHE, THINK, STRUGGLE, LOVE

The Verbs of Prayer

With a certain philological liberty, Giacomo Leopardi in his *Zibaldone* (1817–1832) connected "to meditate" with the Latin *medeor*, "to medicate": this would be, therefore, a sort of medicine of the soul. Prayerful meditation is certainly a requirement of faith, so much so that prayer is a universal anthropological phenomenon. We will now seek to define a basic map of its structure, showing its vital and personal repercussions. There will be four cardinal points of this guide that will accompany our subsequent spiritual pilgrimage in the Psalter as an epiphany of faith.

The first verb of prayer is physical: *to breathe*, connected—as has been said—to the *os*, the "mouth" that *orat*, "prays." The philosopher Søren Kierkegaard (1813–1855) had no hesitation when he noted in his *Diary*: "The ancients rightly said that prayer is breathing. This shows how foolish it is to talk about the reason why one must pray. Why do I breathe? Because otherwise I would die. It is the same

3

way with prayer." The theologian and cardinal Yves Congar (1904–1995), in his work *The Ways of the Living God*, reiterated this theme: "With prayer we receive oxygen to breathe. With the sacraments we nourish ourselves. But before nourishment is breath, and the breath is prayer." The soul that reduces prayer to the minimum remains asphyxiated; if it excludes all invocation, it is slowly strangled. If one lives in an environment of foul air, all of life is saddened; this is what happens with prayer, which needs a pure atmosphere, free from outside distractions, haloed in silence.

This shows the necessity of creating a clear inner horizon in which it may be possible to contemplate, meditate, reflect, and turn toward the light of God. The use of this physical symbolism to define prayer is interesting. It often pervades the Psalms, which often create a counterpoint between "soul" and "throat," because there is one Hebrew word for both, *nefesh*: "The soul/throat thirsts for God, for the living God . . . My God, my God, from the dawn I desire you alone, my soul / throat thirsts for you, my flesh desires you in an arid and thirsty land without water" (Ps 42:2; 63:1). Saint Paul reiterated this physicality, which is not merely organic, because we do not *have* a body, we *are* a body: "Present your bodies as a living sacrifice, holy and acceptable to God, which is your spiritual worship" (Rm 12:1). We must, therefore, rediscover the spontaneity and constancy of the explicit and implicit breath of prayer, like the woman of the Song of Solomon in that stupendous confession of love, made up of only four words in Hebrew: *anî jeshenah welibbî 'er*, "I slept, but my heart was awake" (Song 5:2). Faith, like love, does not take up only a few hours of existence, but is its soul, its constant breathing.

"Prayer is to religion what thought is to philosophy. The religious sense prays just as organ of thought thinks." Thus the German Romantic poet Novalis is quoted incisively in the same language by the philosopher Martin Heidegger (1889–1976), although in reverse, *denken ist danken*, "to think is to thank." The second cardinal point is, therefore, to think. Prayer is not a simple emotion, it must involve reason and will, reflection and passion, truth and action. In this regard Saint Thomas Aquinas considered "prayer as an act of reason that applies the desire of the will to He who is not in our power but is superior to us, meaning God."

The figure of Mary, sketched by the evangelist Luke (2:19), after having lived the experience of divine maternity, is exemplary: she "treasures the words" and the events experienced, and in her heart, or in her mind and conscience, there "meditates" upon them. In Greek she gathers them into a transcendent unity (*symbállousa*), and this is true "thought" according to God. The interweaving of prayer and faith presumes precisely a constant decanting between these two actions, because of which one invokes the one who is known. Thus it is precisely in praying that the Psalmist can affirm that "In Judah God is known" (Ps 76:1, RSV). The "I" of the praying person encounters and dialogues with the divine "I AM," revealed on Sinai in the burning bush (Ex 3:14). The one who prays knows God and, in his light, knows himself, as suggested by another philosopher, Ludwig Wittgenstein, in his notes from 1914–1916: "Praying is thinking about the meaning of life."

There is, however, a third and surprising cardinal point of prayer: it is *struggling*. One thinks immediately of the nighttime scene in the Bible that takes place on the banks of the Jabbok, a tributary of the Jordan (Gen 32:23–33). There Jacob duels with the mysterious Being who in the end remains the Unknown, but is so powerful as to change Jacob's name to Israel, thus changing his life and his mission. He is also the one who strikes him and dislocates his thigh, injuring him therefore in his very existence, and it is he who blesses him by entrusting him to a new history ("The sun rose upon him as he passed Penuel . . ."[Gn 32:31, RSV]). Now, it is curious to note that the prophet Hosea interpreted this experience of the biblical patriarch as an invocation of God, and therefore as a prayer: "He strove with the angel and prevailed, he wept and sought his favor" (Hos 12:4, RSV). We must devote more attention to this dimension of prayer and faith, because the dominant form of Psalmic prayer is precisely "supplication."

This dimension of prayer gushes forth from suffering; it becomes a heartrending plea addressed to God. It experiences also the divine silence and absence. It is incarnated in the Psalmic cry repeated by Christ on the cross: "My God, my God, why have you abandoned me?" It is reproduced in the continual protest of Job, who reaches the point of feeling that God is a beast: "he has gnashed his teeth at me; my adversary sharpens his eyes against me. . . . he seized me by the neck and dashed me to pieces; he set me up as his target, his archers slashes open my kidneys without mercy; ... He breaks me with breach upon breach; he runs upon me like a warrior" (Job 16:9, 12).

It is that "contending/fighting" with God which already explained the name "Israel" according to the Bible (Gn 32:29) and which Job reiterates in his incessant lamentation: "It is with the Almighty that I wish to speak, it is with God that I desire to contend" (Job 13:3). And again, that night of the spirit which enfolds great mystics like Saint John of the Cross, who however in the famous stanzas of his *Spiritual Canticle*, beginning precisely on the basis of the obscure absence, leads us to the last luminous cardinal point, that of the loving presence and the intimate embrace: "Where have you hidden yourself, O Beloved, leaving me in tears? Like the stag you fled, after wounding me: I went out after you calling, and you had gone away . . ."

Finally, there is the encounter: the fourth verb of prayer is *to love*. This delineates the supreme goal of prayer and of faith, which is expressed through the other dominant genre of the Psalter, next to that of supplication: trusting and joyful praise. Some forms of spirituality put more emphasis on the divine transcendence and inaccessibility, which must be contemplated, admired, celebrated, but is hard to love. The ancient Sumerians sang to the god Enlil for "his many perfections that bring astonishment," while knowing that he was "like a tangled skein that no one can unravel, a tangle of thread with no end in sight." Islam also exalts the unattainable divine glory, a blinding sun that at its height leaves a reflection in the puddle of water that is man. And yet, the authentic harbor of prayer is intimacy between the believer and his God, so much so that Muslim spirituality itself tends toward this embrace. In fact, Rabi'a, a mystic of Basra of the eighth century, sang under the starry firmament of the Orient: "My Lord, in the sky shine the stars, the eyes of lovers close. Every woman in love is alone with her beloved. And I am alone here with you."

In the Christian faith intimacy is complete because God is invoked as "abba," "daddy," in the supreme *oratio dominica*, the Our Father, chosen by Jesus as the distinctive prayer of the Christian. With this there is not only a God *about whom* to speak, but *to whom* to speak in a dialogue in which there is an exchange of glances. This is the moment of silent prayer: "contemplate him and you will be radiant," the Psalmist sings (34:5). It is the same experience of the lovers who, after a spoken conversation, look into each others' eyes. And this is the more intense and sweet language, more true and intimate, as Pascal suggested, convinced that in faith as in love, "silences are more eloquent than words."

Let us put ourselves, then, in that same attitude as the biblical worshiper of Psalm 123, in a delicate and tender exchange of glances between the believer and his God: "To thee I lift up my eyes, O thou who art enthroned in the heavens! Behold, as the eyes of servants look to the hand of their master . . . so our eyes look to the Lord our God, till he have mercy upon us" (vv. 1–2, RSV). It is in this silent meeting of the eyes that prayerful contemplation arises.

CHAPTER II

AT THE SPRINGS OF THE JORDAN OF THE SPIRIT

The God of Grace and of the Word

In her book *Waiting for God*, the extraordinary French Jewish thinker Simone Weil (1909–1943) reminded us that it is illusory to want to rise up to heaven with ever higher leaps, and added: "If we look long at heaven, God comes down and carries us away. As Aeschylus says, that which is divine is without strain." This, an evocative parable to extol the primacy of divine grace, is Pauline *cháris*, a Greek word at the root of the Latin *caritas*, and while it expresses love it also produced the modern word, *charm*, evoking the allure and the beauty of this gift. "No one can come to me unless the Father who sent me draws him," Jesus says in his grandiose "Eucharistic" discourse in Capernaum (Jn 6:44, RSV).

From this theological spring begins our spiritual pilgrimage in the horizon of prayer, *lex et ars credendi*, the norm and splendor of faith. It will be a voyage that selects one route from among the many possible: as has already

9

been said, we will take the path that crosses the land of the Psalms. We will venture into the 150 poetical texts that make up the Psalter, select many of the 19,531 Hebrew words that are the voice of the ancient worshipers, follow the various literary and thematic registers, savor the symbols, the images, and the sentiments, share the joys and sorrows, the faith and questioning, experience the trust and abandonment to God, but also the fear and silence, extract "a song every day, a song for every day," because prayer is "the recompense of being men," to use an expression from Abraham J. Heschel (1907–1972), a Jewish philosopher and mystic, in his book *Who Is Man?*

In one of his *Enarrationes super Psalmos*, the one dedicated to Psalm 137, almost interrupting the course of his thoughts, Saint Augustine exclaimed "*Psalterium meum, gaudium meum*," and he demonstrated this joy in the very depths of the little ocean of writing that he left to us: of the more than twenty thousand Old Testament passages (out of the sixty thousand from the Bible as a whole) that Augustine cites, no fewer than 11,500 come from the Psalter. With this profound inner adherence let us contemplate in our first stage the spring of that Jordan of the spirit which we will follow later. One of the Psalms at the highest poetic and spiritual level, Psalm 42, which we have already evoked and will meet again, has as its background precisely the cataract springs of that river, at the foot of the Hermon: "I remember you Lord from the land of Jordan and of Hermon . . . Deep calls to deep at the thunder of your cataracts; all thy waves and thy billows have gone over me" (vv. 6–8).

We will make our start there because the spring of prayer and faith is the divine grace that reveals itself. In the beginning there is theophany, there is revelation, there is that gift of love which makes our hearts tremble in faith and moves our lips in prayer. God precedes and exceeds all of our invocations, as Saint Paul himself says in citing with amazement a prophetic saying: "Then Isaiah is so bold as to say, 'I have made myself to be found by those who did not seek me; I have shown myself to those who did not ask for me'" (Rm 10:20; cf. Is 65:1). On the facade of his residence in Küssnacht near Zurich, Carl Gustav Jung (1875–1961), one of the fathers of psychoanalysis, placed this Latin epigraph: *Vocatus atque non vocatus, Deus aderit*—"both to those who turn to him and to those who ignore him, God will always be present."

And yet, the first divine epiphany is precisely that of his Word. The Bible itself opens with the voice of the Creator that splits the silence of nothingness: "In the beginning . . . God said, 'Let there be light'; and there was light" (Gn 1:1, 3, RSV). In conceptual terms, the New Testament opens with the hymn of the prologue of John: "In the beginning was the Word . . . and the Word was God" (Jn 1:1, RSV). The divine word also shatters the neutral flow of time, creating salvation history. The main experience of Sinai, from the pinnacle of which come the ten commandments of the Lord, is summarized by Moses as follows: "Then the Lord spoke to you out of the midst of the fire; you heard the sound of words, but saw no form; there was only a voice" (Dt 4:12, RSV). The Word of God now resounds in Scripture, in particular, in the Torah.

The invitation that is issued to us by the longest of the Psalms, number 119, traditionally used by the Catholic liturgy to mark the passing hours of the day, is precisely that of listening to the divine word present in the Bible. Like an Eastern melopoiea that rises upward in a spiral, but always echoing and recreating fixed motifs, or like the waves that always flow over the same place on shore but in ceaselessly changing forms, this immense alphabetical canticle—which the philosopher and believer Pascal recited every day—celebrates the beauty and power of the Word of God that is also called "law, testimony, judgment, saying, decree, precept, order." A true spirituality must, therefore, always be founded on the Word of God. The Fathers of the Church were exemplary in this. As has been said, they did not speak about the Bible, but they spoke the Bible itself: the very fabric of their texts, the spirit of their message, the soul of their reflections and meditations was constantly made up of the divine word.

In the verses of Psalm 119 we feel the vibration of love for this Word that shines in the mist or the darkness of existence. In fact, "thy word is a lamp to my feet, Lord a light to my path" (v. 105). When one proceeds in darkness it is easy to stumble, but if one holds a torch, the outlines of the path become visible and one can avoid the rocks along the way and get a glimpse of the destination. "The unfolding of thy words gives light . . . Thy promise is well tried" (vv. 130, 140, RSV). It is a word that infuses sweetness into the heart, melting the ice of sadness and the bitterness of dissatisfaction, giving flavor to a monotonous existence: "How sweet are thy promises to my palate, sweeter than honey to my mouth!" (v. 103; cf. Ps 19:10). It is a word that helps us to rebuild the true scale of values, which is often calibrated only upon things, money, power: "I love thy commandments above gold, above fine gold" (v. 127, RSV).

In the end those who follow this shining light, who taste the savor and admire the preciousness of the divine word explode in a profession of love that summarizes almost in a sigh the impassioned declaration of the woman in the Song of Solomon. She, in fact, in a parallel double verse marked by the rhythmic repetition of the two personal pronouns of the couple, ô, "he, his," and î, "I, mine," sung in Hebrew: *dodî lî wa'anî lô . . . 'anî ledodî wedodî lî*, "my beloved is mine and I am his . . . I am my beloved's and my beloved is mine" (Song 2:16; 6:3, RSV). The believer who has listened to the Word turns to his Lord and simply exclaims: *lekâ-'anî hôshî'enî*, "I am thine, save me" (Ps 119:94, RSV).

By allowing oneself to be won over by this song of the Word of God, by its rhythm similar to that of musical "perpetual motion," by repeating this sort of biblical rosary dominated by the repetition typical of the language of lovers, one becomes drawn into, enfolded in, and even swept away by its liberating power and becomes an obedient and practicing listener: "Blessed are those who hear the word of God and keep it!" (Lk 11:28, RSV). Then one can proceed with trust through the days, without the anxiety and discontent that in no fewer than six passages of the Sermon on the Mount Jesus sought to dispel from the horizon of his disciple's life: "Do not be anxious about your life . . ." (Mt 6:25–34, RSV).

In front of us and before us stands the Lord, the shepherd who guides us. We would like, then, to conclude his contemplation on the primacy of God, on his grace, on his love, and on his Word, with a famous Psalmic song of faith and trust, Psalm 23. Of this the philosopher Henri Bergson (1859–1941) wrote: "The hundreds of books that I have read have never brought me such light and such comfort as these verses." The path winds through the desert, with all of the tension created by a voyage through the harsh solitude of the steppes. In front of the flock advances the shepherd, whose distinctive signs, the staff and crook, stand out against the sky like a sure point of reference, because he knows how to avoid the dangerous detours and valleys.

To this first symbol is added another that also constitutes the arrival point of the voyage: that of the supper and the host. "Thou preparest a table before me . . . thou anointest my head with oil, my cup overflows." (v. 5, RSV). This is, then, a further step: the grace/*cháris* of the shepherd that illuminates us and guides us in the truth is revealed in the end to be grace/*caritas*, meaning communion, intimacy, love, expressed precisely by the symbol of the table. This can evoke, among other things, the sacrifice of communion that included a sacred meal in the temple: the dream of the devotee is nothing less than to "dwell in the house of the Lord for ever" (v. 6, RSV), beside his God.

This closes the first stage of our journey through the Psalms. In it is unveiled before us the epiphany of God and of his Word. Man is not a solitary vagabond without a guide. The thematic and structural center of Psalm 23 is in fact placed in a clear declaration: *kî 'attah 'immadî*, "because you are with me." There is a presence that keeps watch beside us, there is a word that gives meaning to the journey of life, there is a God who does not let fall from his hands the creature that he has shaped and that still bears the warmth and imprint of those fingers.

The theologian Karl Barth (1886–1968) was right when he modified by only one letter the famous motto of Descartes. The French philosopher, with his *Cogito, ergo sum*, "I think, therefore I am," had centered on the conscious ego the whole of the human being who establishes himself in his identity. The German theologian, instead, introduced a variation that was slight and yet able to generate a Copernican revolution of biblical stamp: *Cogitor, ergo sum*, "I am thought of/loved, therefore I am." I am certain that God has discovered me, but I must confess that I am not always certain that I have discovered God. Faith is above all a gift, even if— as we will see—it is at the same time an accomplishment. Once again Saint Paul is very clear: "You have come to know God, or rather you have come to be known by God" (Gal 4:9). In the Bible "to know" is also "to love."

CHAPTER III

THE SONG OF THE TWOFOLD SUN

God the Creator

"Just as those who have gone out to sea in a boat are seized by an immense anguish in entrusting a scrap of wood to the immensity of the waves, so also we suffer as we dare to venture upon such a vast ocean of mysteries." This was the confession of Origen, a great Christian writer of the third century, while he was embarking upon the exegesis of the book of Genesis. His emotion reverberates in each one of us when, on a starry night, we contemplate the Milky Way with its billions of stars or when, in the wake of scientific research, we wonder to ourselves about the "multiverse" that now makes paradoxically narrow our nonetheless immense universe. The vast and stunning silences of outer space are, however, symbolically shattered by the song of faith.

In fact, as the Judaeo-Hellenistic author of the book of Wisdom already suggested, "from the greatness and beauty of created things by analogy is contemplated their author." (Wis 13:5). St. Paul was also convinced that "the invisible perfections (of God)—or his eternal power and divinity—come to be contemplated and understood from the Creator of the whole world through the works he has accomplished " (Rm 1:20). With a play on words, the Judaeo-Alexandrian philosopher Philo reminded us that the *poiémata*, the created works of God, are also his *poiémata*, his poems, the messages he has sent to humanity. This is the same approach that is taken by the Psalmic prayer that celebrates the second great theophany, that of the Creator who works precisely through his first epiphany, the Word.

In fact, unlike the Eastern cosmogonies, like the Mesopotamian *Enuma Elish*, which considered the act of creation a divine battle in which the creator god Marduk made the creation blossom from the lacerated remains of the defeated divinity Tiamat, the biblical Genesis introduces the imperative voice of the Creator who from nothing—represented by the *tohu wabohu*, the chaos and darkness of the empty abyss—makes being appear. The Psalmist sings: "By the word of the Lord the heavens were made, and all their host by the breath of his mouth" (Ps 33:6, RSV). As in the scene painted by Michelangelo in the Sistine Chapel, the Creator dominates the creation that is "the work of his hands" and that therefore preserves in itself the imprint of a transcendent plan.

For the worshiper, being is therefore not simply "nature" but "creation," "cosmos," meaning harmony, order, design, albeit in its complexity and in its immeasurable and even indecipherable contours. The universe contains—as suggested by a great exegete of the Psalter, Hermann Gunkel (1862–1932)—a "silent theological music," a message that knows no audible words or echoes and that nonetheless permeates everything. It is what is proclaimed by Psalm 19: "The heavens narrate the glory of God; and the firmament proclaims the works of his hand" (v. 1). Outer space is, therefore, personified as an enthusiastic witness of the creative work of God, it is a "narrator," a herald of his glorious power.

The psalmist continues: "Day to day pours forth speech, and night to night declares knowledge" (v. 2, RSV). So even the circadian rhythm bears a proclamation in itself: day and night are anthropomorphically depicted as messengers that transmit from station to station the great news of creation. Space and time are therefore caught up in a real and proper "*kerygma*," in a gospel of light and joy, communicated "without language, without words, without their voice being heard, and yet through all the earth their proclamation goes out and to the ends of the world their message" (vv. 3–4). The inner gaze of man and his attentive ear can, however, decipher this secret harmony. The apparently mute world reveals itself to be speaking to the ear of the spirit: this is what the theologian and cardinal Jean Daniélou called the "cosmic revelation" open to all of humanity.

Saint John Chrysostom commented: "This silence of the heavens is a voice more resonant than that of a trumpet; this voice cries out to our eyes and not to our ears of the greatness of the one who made them." A synagogue song for the feast of *Shavuʿôt*, or Pentecost, imagines that between heaven and earth there is in reality spread out a parchment on which the Creator has written a message to which humanity can respond by inserting its alleluia of praise and thanksgiving. It is no coincidence that in Psalm 148 twenty-two earthy creatures are called together, as many as the letters of the Hebrew alphabet, so that under the guidance of the man who is the liturgist of this rite they may intone an Alleluia in the cosmic temple that has as its apse the heavens, and the last line of the Psalter literally invites "everything that breathes" to give praise to the Lord (Ps 150:6, RSV).

Biblical faith, therefore, although it assigns—as we will see—primacy to time and therefore to history as the setting of divine revelation, also presents space not as a neutral reality, but as an epiphanic horizon where God is present, through which we creatures "live and move and have our being" in him, to use the famous declaration of Saint Paul in the Areopagus of Athens (Acts 17:28, RSV). In the face of creation, which the Psalter depicts a number of times as a multicolored tapestry of marvels (see for example the wonderful "canticle of the creatures" present in Psalm 104, or the delicious springtime idyll of Psalm 65:10–14, or the startling "Psalm of the seven thunderclaps," number 29, which introduces a violent tempest), the worshiper is invited to a not merely romantic but a theological contemplation. This is what is suggested by the biblical sage called Sirach in concluding the grandiose mystical geography in chapters 42 and 43 of his book: "We could say much and we will never finish but the conclusion of the speech will be 'He is the all'" (43:27).

Years ago, on a warm May afternoon, I was in front of a church on the outskirts of Milan before a confirmation celebration. There were some other adults with me, and the pastor. A little girl came up to us and insisted that we look at a crack in the pavement of the street: a tiny strawberry plant had miraculously sprouted there. Only the one who has a pure eye is able to discover the little wonders and not tread on them without noticing. The English writer Gilbert Keith Chesterton (1874–1936) was convinced that "the world will never starve for want of wonders, but for want of wonder." The absence of astonishment on the part of contemporary man, superficial or bent only over the works of his own hands, incapable of lifting his eyes to heaven and admiring in profundity the two extremes of the universe and of the microcosm, has made it such that the creation entrusted to him has often been humiliated and devastated.

Instead of "cultivating and caring for" the earth as delegated by the Creator, he has behaved like a tyrant who defaces the divine plan, and is no longer able to listen to the secret message concealed in creatures. A spirituality that ignores the earthly horizon, that is unable to enjoy the beauty of its forms and the richness of its fruits, which almost invites one to abstract oneself by detaching from creation in favor of disembodied intimacy, does not belong to vigorous biblical realism and the Christian incarnation. An interesting rabbinical aphorism admonishes that at the end of our lives we will be judged in part on the just and licit pleasures and enjoyments that we have not lived to the full. Authentic ascesis is not only negation, but is also harmony between body and spirit, it is renunciation and exercise for a genuine fullness.

In looking out with astonishment upon the divine epiphany of the cosmos, we are presented again with all of the greatness, but also with all of the tensions, of the dialogue between faith and science. The famous father of quantum physics, Max Planck (1858–1947), affirmed in his work *The Knowledge of the Physical World*: "Science and religion are not in contrast, but need each other to complete one another in the mind of the man who thinks seriously." Science, in fact, is dedicated to the "stage" of being, to the phenomenon, to the facts and figures, to the "how"; religion, instead, is consecrated to the "foundation," to the ultimate sense of being, to the "why."

Science and religion are "non-overlapping" magisteriums, as the scientist Stephen J. Gould (1941–2002) said, they are autonomous paths with their own statutes, protocols, and methods. They are distinct but not totally separate, because their object is the same, although they have different approaches. Giovanni Battista Montini, when he was still a young priest, wrote these words to the professors and students of Catholic universities: "Charity and truth are not enemies; nor are science and faith, human thought and divine thought, extreme critical elaboration and extreme mystical elaboration."

The believer, therefore, finds himself before the necessity of flying through the infinite spaces of being and existence with the two wings of faith and reason, to use the well-known image with which John Paul II begins *Fides et Ratio*. Pascal, a great philosopher, scientist, and believer, warned against the two extremes to be avoided: "excluding reason, not admitting anything but reason," and elsewhere he noted that "human things must be understood to be loved, while divine things must be loved to be understood." There are, in fact, mysteries in which one must have the courage to immerse oneself, to plumb the depths in order to understand them, a little like what happens to those who dive into the ocean to swim, certain that the water will open in front of them. And it is in this navigation that territory is conquered, that one aspires to what is beyond, that one overcomes fear. There are realities in which one must believe first in order to understand them. This is the way of prayer and of theology that intuits and encounters the mystery of the divine and then seeks to penetrate and decipher it. It is a way that proceeds by counterpoint, but not by opposition, with that of science that demands verification and analysis before all adherence and synthesis.

The harmony between the two paths is symbolically extolled also in Psalm 19, which we have chosen as emblematic. This hymn, in fact, is constructed as a diptych, dedicated to a twofold sun. The first is the star that blazes in the sky, described as a bridegroom who at dawn leaves his nuptial chamber and turns into a hero or an athlete who travels his orbit in triumph, enfolding creation in his warmth and light (vv. 4–6). But there is a second star that shines in the heaven of the spirit, and it is the Torah, the Word of God described with solar images: "The commandments of the Lord are radiant, enlightening the eyes . . . the Word of God is pure, your servant is enlightened" (v. 8). The sun blazes in the height of heaven, all the earth is enfolded in its ardor, the air is immobile, no corner can escape its light. The Word of God, instead, irradiates its splendor into the horizon of the conscience, melts its ice, pours into it light and hope. The medieval rabbinical exegete Kimchi commented: "Just as the world cannot develop or live without the action of the sun, so also the soul cannot develop and reach its fullness of life without the Torah."

The two divine epiphanies we have considered so far, of the word and of creation, intersect in Psalm 19. After the revealing Word of God comes his creating Word. This invites us to pause before the sunrises and sunsets, before the "snow that comes down like wool, the frost that is spread like dust" (Ps 147:16), before "the sea, great and wide" (Ps 104:25, RSV) and so on, in a kaleidoscope of scenes that the poets of the Psalms make pass before our astonished eyes. "When thou sendest forth thy Spirit, they are created; and thou renewest the face of the ground" (Ps 104:30, RSV). Let above all stop before the living creatures: the Lord "holds in his hand the soul of every living thing and the breath of every human being" (Job 12:10). It is evocative, this icon of the Creator who holds in his hand the end of the thread of breath that comes from the mouth of every one of his living creatures.

Before the creation in its variety and richness, we can then lift up our thanksgiving to God for our existence and his many wonders. We as well can echo the "You song" that the Hasidim, the "pious," the Jews of Central Europe intoned in contemplating their landscape, even when this was overshadowed by the terror of the pogrom, the anti-Semitic massacres: "Wherever I may go, You; wherever I may stop, You; only You, still You, always You. Heaven You, earth You. Wherever I turn and look, only You, still You, always You."

CHAPTER IV

THE SPARROWS AND SWALLOWS OF THE TEMPLE

The God of the Liturgy

"The world is like the eye: the ocean is the white, the land is the iris, Jerusalem is the pupil, and the image reflected in it is the temple." This interesting map of the world, proposed by a Jewish aphorism, leads us to the third theophany that the Psalter presents to us, after that of the Word and of creation. It is as if we were proceeding by concentric circles, from the immense circle of the universe or multiverse to our planet; the objective is then narrowed to the Promised Land. But even more delimited is the perimeter of the holy city, Jerusalem; one last zoom focuses on the hills of Zion and here we discover the center, or rather the beating heart of the space of prayer, the temple. "O Lord," the Psalmist confesses, "I love the house in which you dwell . . . , and the place where your glory is present . . . To your servants the stones of Zion are dear" (Ps 26:8; 102:15).

Ours now becomes a true pilgrimage toward the *'ohel mo'ed*, the "tent of the encounter," as the Bible calls the sanctuary on its sacred summit, the place in which the believer finds the assembly (*qahal* in Hebrew, *ekklesía* in Greek) that has been called together by God. In fact, in that highly restricted circle He whom "not even the heavens and the heavens of heavens can contain" (1 Ks 8:27) allows himself to be "compressed" in order to encounter the human creature who is a prisoner within the limits of space. Solomon, in the grandiose prayer of consecration for the temple of Zion, evokes precisely this divine promise: *Shemî sham*, "my name shall be there," which means that the divine person is there and reveals himself, he speaks and embraces his faithful (1 Ks 8:29, RSV).

In fact, the prophet Zephaniah, in a little "psalm" embedded in his brief book, transfigures this affirmation with a tender and delicate image. Zion, "metro-poli," or city-mother, hosts within itself a glorious maternity: "King of Israel is the Lord *beqirbek* . . . The Lord, your God, is *beqirbek*," literally "in your womb" (1 Ks 3:15, 17). A presence that is living, gentle, sensitive, joyous ("He will rejoice over you with gladness, he will renew you in his love" [1 Ks 3:17, RSV]). This is almost a prefiguration of the divine maternity of Mary, who—as Saint Ambrose said— "is not the God of the temple, but the temple of God."

This maternal face of Zion takes on a universal profile in Psalm 87, the "birth" song of humanity, marked three times by the formula *jullad sham/bah*, "is born there / in it" (vv. 4–6). This was a locution of a legal character that declared the native citizenship of a person in a particular city. So then, in the spiritual registry of Zion are now inscribed all of the peoples of the earth delineated through the four cardinal points: Rahab, or Egypt, is the western power, Babylon embodies the eastern pole, Tyre is the northern commercial center, while Palestine/Philistia defines the south.

It is an extraordinary "ecumenical" vision, which sees streaming into Zion with singing and dancing all of the peoples of the earth, who are crying out joyfully: "All my springs are in you!" (v. 7, RSV). Psalm 87, which retraces the universalistic spirit of prophets like Isaiah (2:1–5; 19:18–25; 56:1–7; 60:3–11; 66:18–21), thus becomes the ideal hymn of the Church in the wake of the Pauline affirmation: "The Jerusalem above is free, and she is our mother" (Gal 4:26, RSV). *Lumen Gentium* confirms that "at the end of time [the Church] will gloriously achieve completion, when, as is read in the Fathers, all the just, from Adam and 'from Abel, the just one, to the last of the elect,' will be gathered together with the Father in the universal Church." (no. 2).

We too, therefore, set out as pilgrims climbing to "the city of our God! His holy mountain, beautiful in elevation, the city of the great King" (Ps 48:1–2, RSV), intoning the "songs of ascent," or Psalms 120–134. "Our feet have been standing within your gates, O Jerusalem" (122:2, RSV); the gaze is lifted to the cornices of the temple where one glimpses the nests of the birds, and from the mouth bursts forth an exclamation: "Even the sparrow finds a home, and the swallow a nest for herself, where she may lay her young, at thy altars, O Lord of hosts, my King and my God. Blessed is the man who finds refuge in you and has your ways in his heart" (Ps 84:3–5).

In the temple, which is the site of the cultic theophany, the revelation of God during the liturgy, we would like to pause for a brief and essential reflection on the reality that acts as a constant background to the entire Psalter, meaning the liturgy, and on its fundamental theological structure. In it man and God actually encounter each other, the one with his existence and praise, the other with his grace and salvation.

The French writer Paul Claudel (1868–1955)—who received the illumination of his conversion at vespers in Notre-Dame in Paris—wrote to his colleague Jacques Rivière, an agnostic seeker: "The liturgy and assiduous attendance at the celebrations of the Church will teach you more than books. Immerse yourself in this immense bath of glory, of certitude, of poetry."

There are two fundamental coordinates for every liturgical celebration. The first is "horizontal" and concerns the assembly that comes to the temple, and it is expressed well through what are called "entrance liturgies." This is, in practice, the opening penitential act of our Eucharistic liturgy. The procession is at the threshold of the temple and the Levites demand from the faithful an examination of conscience before crossing that boundary: "Who shall ascend the hill of the Lord? And who shall stand in his holy place He who has clean hands and a pure heart, who does not lift up his soul to what is false, and does not swear deceitfully" (Ps 24:3–4, RSV).

Exemplary in this regard is Psalm 15. In it, the Levites (most likely) are listing the prerequisite conditions for entering into the holy atmosphere of the temple. Unlike the traditional ritual demands of external purity, of decorous behavior and decent dress, they present—in the spirit of the prophetic "*kerygma*," the proclamation of a radical bond between faith and life, between worship and justice (Is 1:10–20, for example)—eleven prescriptions of a primarily moral nature.

As the Talmud noted, "David reduced to eleven all of the 613 commandments of the Torah," and if we would like to continue, Christ reduced the eleven to just two precepts, or rather to only one: "You shall love the Lord your God . . . You shall love your neighbor" (Mt 22:34–40, RSV).

This sequence can today become for us as well a sort of blueprint for the examination of conscience prior to reconciliation with God in the sacrament of penance or at the moment of silent personal reflection before the liturgy of the Word and the Eucharist. The first of the three requirements is of a general nature: "to walk with integrity," or to live a just life, "the practice of justice" and "the truth of the heart." It is a spiritual and existential fundamental option.

There then follows a list of eight concrete responsibilities that concerns social life: the fight against slander, respect of neighbor, the protection of the dignity of the person, the rejection of all collusion with evil, the choice of the good and of faith, the rejection of all fraud, the elimination of usury, the removal of the scourge of corruption. This is a warning to be repeated still today to ourselves and to the faithful, otherwise worship becomes an external rite, a celebration, of a farce—and God, as Isaiah says, detests offerings and sacrifices, he averts his eyes from hands that are raised in prayer but bloodied because he cannot "endure iniquity and solemn assembly" (1:13, RSV).

Jesus has also left us his entrance liturgy centered on that one commandment of love: "If you are offering your gift at the altar, and there remember that your brother has something against you, leave your gift there before the altar and go; first be reconciled to your brother, and then come and offer your gift" (Mt 5:23–24, RSV). Saint Paul later applied this as a condition of Christ explicitly and strictly to the Eucharistic liturgy: "Whoever, therefore, eats the bread or drinks the cup of the Lord in an unworthy manner will be guilty of profaning the body and blood of the Lord. Let a man examine himself, and so eat of the bread and drink of the cup. For any one who eats and drinks without discerning the body eats and drinks judgment upon himself" (1 Cor 11:27–29, RSV).

It is under this indispensable precondition of humility in the confession of faults that one can cross the threshold that leads to communion with the Lord of justice and of truth, with the "God who is light and in whom there is no darkness whatsoever" (1 Jn 1:5). Unfortunately, we often treat the penitential act as nothing more than a hurried ritual gesture that does not touch the heart. Marshall McLuhan (1911–1980), a very well-known expert of modern mass communication, who had gone through a journey of conversion, observed ironically: "One enters the church kneeling and in silence. Instead there is the tendency to go straight to the pulpit."

There is, however, another fundamental and primary dimension of the liturgy. It is "vertical" and invites us to recognize the presence of God himself and of his epiphany of the liturgy. Of course, we must shake hands in fraternal charity, but our gaze and our hearts must then be turned upward, toward God and his Christ. In fact, the protagonist in worship is the Lord with his presence: if he were to make himself absent, the temple would be reduced to a building of more or less decorous architecture, and the celebration to a ceremony more or less folkloric. It is revealing that in Hebrew one speaks of the Shekinah, the divine "Presence," as the very soul of the temple, and perhaps John in his hymnic prologue tips a wink at this term when he speaks of the Word who "pitches his tent among us" (Jn 1:14), in Greek *eskénosen*, a verb that includes the root s-k-n. The "flesh," or the humanity of Christ, is the supreme throne of the Shekinah, it is the perfect tent, the living temple of the encounter with the Father.

So then, in the temple of Sion the Lord waits for the worshiper, and there are many ritual references which evoke this embrace of intimacy. We would like to cite only two symbols that celebrate the divine proximity to his servants "who stand by night in the house of the Lord" (Ps 134:1), awaiting the light of dawn, a sign of the revelation destined for the worshiper.

The first is that of the *rock*: "I love thee, O Lord, my strength, my rock, my fortress, my shield, my powerful salvation my stronghold" (Ps 18:1–2). This litany of divine titles, which opens a canticle almost certainly to be attributed to David, expresses with great clarity the stability that the Lord gives to his faithful in the temple. The idea—perhaps taken from the image of the sheltering rock—of the immunity guaranteed to the one who then sought the right of asylum in the sacred precincts, becomes a proclamation of serenity in the whirlwind of trials and the siege of evil. From the lips of the worshiper there springs, therefore, this prayer: "The Lord is my light and my salvation, whom shall I fear? The Lord is the stronghold of my life, of whom shall I be afraid?" (Ps 27:1, RSV). This is a gift that is particularly necessary in our contemporary experience, marked—as is commonly said—by a "fluidity" that makes everything mobile, insubstantial, volatile. The mind wanders in the vacuum of thought, the heart entrusts itself to the flux of the emotions, morality knows no objective norms, but only spontaneous and instinctive choices. The experience of the encounter with God, his Word, and his presence in the liturgy, create, on the other hand, solidity, stability, firmness, and truth.

The other metaphor of the divine Shekinah is that of the *wings,* which runs throughout the Psalter with this invocation: "Protect me in the shadow of thy wings" (Ps 17:8). They are the wings of the cherubim of the ark and those of an eagle in the exodus from Egypt: "Like an eagle that watches over its nest, that flutters over its young, he (the Lord) spread out his wings, and bore them on his pinions" (Dt 32:11). Very tender is the song of Psalm 91, which has as its protagonist he "who dwells in the shelter of the Most High, who abides in the shadow of the Almighty": he is certain that the Lord "will cover you with his pinions, and under his wings you will find refuge" (vv. 1, 4, RSV). It is a hymn in which one breathes an almost maternal atmosphere, the embrace dispels every terror of night and day.

In *Doctor Zhivago*, Boris Pasternak (1890–1960) recalled that this Psalm, written on a scrap of paper, was worn by soldiers over their hearts, in the certainty—as the text says—that "no evil shall befall you," neither "the terror of the night" nor "the arrow that flies by day" (vv. 10,5). It is evocative to enter sometimes, during the daytime, into those churches that face the noisy streets of the city and there, in the shadows and in the silence, see a person who is alone before his Lord. He needs nothing but that encounter which gives serenity and peace amid the bustle of life.

Now let us leave behind the temple and its liturgy, the place of the third theophany, where "my prayer rises like incense before you, O Lord, my lifted hands like an evening sacrifice" (Ps 141:2). Outside, life is in full swing in the crowded squares, where "old men and old women shall again sit in the streets of Jerusalem, each with staff in hand for very age. And the streets of the city shall be full of boys and girls playing in its streets" (Zc 8:4–5). The Orthodox theologian Pavel Evdokimov (1901–1970) urged that the doors of churches should be kept open so that the wreaths of incense, the echoes of the liturgical chants, the prayerful invocations, borne by the winds of the Spirit of God, should also penetrate the squares and homes where people weep and laugh, hope and despair, work and study, love and hate, even blaspheme and sin. The power of the divine presence that animates the liturgy will be able to fertilize even the desert of history and of human existence.

CHAPTER V

THE RIVER OF TIME

The God of History

A Jewish parable imagines that, when God created the world, he surrounded himself with angels to serve him. One of them carried on a tray ten portions of beauty: the Lord assigned nine of them to Jerusalem, and only one to the rest of the world. Another came forward with the tray of wisdom and its ten quantities: in this case as well, the Creator attributed nine of them to the holy city, and only one to the rest of the earth. And the same was done with many other created gifts. At the end came the angel bearing the great basin of suffering. And here the reader will think that the proportions must be inverted, but instead God cast upon Jerusalem all the same nine portions of suffering, and assigned only one to the rest of humanity. We have mentioned this story because it introduces us to the fourth place where the face of God and his revelation are encountered, after the Word, the creation, and the temple with the liturgy.

This is the horizon in which human history takes place, the river of time: here one experiences joy, celebration, prosperity, laughter, beauty, light, but there are also lurking evil, mourning, sadness, misfortune, tears, the mean and the ugly, darkness. All of these realities are equally distributed in all personal and social affairs, among believers and unbelievers, among men and women, pervading centuries and events. So then, the Bible—in a way that is rather original among all the cultures—emphasizes time as a religious category: you must not seek God first of all in space where however he does show himself, as has been seen, but rather you must discover him above all as he enters human history, becoming truly Emmanuel, God-with-us.

He chooses, then, the reality that is closest to us, that is intrinsic to our existence. In being born, we come out of our mother's uterus to be welcomed by two immense wombs, that of space and that of time. But the latter one attaches itself to us more intimately, above all in its form—as the Greeks said—of *kairós*, the personal experience of time, and not so much that of *chrónos*, or the objective measurement of time that is now made by atomic clocks. God, who alone is the Eternal, compresses himself within human time, which is successive development, and presents himself at the crossroads of history, as well as at the crossroads of space, a bit as happens in the biblical paintings by Chagall that introduce angels and divine presences in the modest everyday life of the *shtetl*, the Jewish village of central Europe.

Gandhi aptly called prayer "the key of the morning and the bolt of the evening." It seeks and encounters God precisely in the life of the person who prays. It finds him in the great events of salvation history, where God walks with his creatures.

With Christianity, prayer discovers him in a man who is also God, Jesus Christ, whose history is therefore infused with the eternal. Finally, it intuits him in the neighbor and in the simple events of everyday life. The God of the Psalter is the Lord of history, which therefore ceases to be simply a nomenclature of dates and facts, but is transformed into sacred history. And this takes place in line with the biblical tradition that professes the "historical Creed." This is proclaimed, for example, by the Jewish believer in the springtime, when he presents at the temple the basket of first fruits (Dt 26:5–9), is presented solemnly by Joshua to all of Israel when they enter the Promised Land at the assembly of Shechem (Judg 24:1–13), and is also sung in the liturgy of the temple of Zion. The Christian Creed is similar to this, being founded on the incarnation of the Son of God in history.

We will now entrust ourselves to a Creed sung in the worship of the temple, reading Psalm 136, which Judaism calls "the Great Hallel," the Paschal hymn of praise for soloist and choir. A Levite soloist comes forward and, after issuing an invitation to praise the "God of gods, the Lord of lords for he is good," he intones in clear terms the events of salvation history in twenty-two couplets, the same as the number of letters in the Hebrew alphabet: it is a joyful summary of all the divine actions and all our words of thanksgiving. The assembly responds to each statement with a fixed antiphon: *kî le'olam hasdô*, "because his love is forever." There appears the term *hesed,* "fidelity, love, grace," which is particularly dear to the Psalter, which uses it 127 times. It is difficult to render the allusive intricacies of this term with just one word in our language.

Hesed, in fact, evokes that indecipherable and inexhaustible atmosphere of intimacy which circulates between two persons who love each other. It is for this reason that it would become the flagship term for the covenant between the Lord and his people. A covenant that in the Bible had initially been modeled on the political-diplomatic treaties between a great king and the princes of lesser states, but that the prophets—beginning with Hosea, in the wake of his marital experience and beleaguered family—had transformed into a pact of love and intimacy, while Jeremiah (31:31–34) and Ezekiel (11:17–20; 36:24–25) had reached the summit of communion between God and creature in proposing a "new" covenant made up of a union of hearts between the Lord and man.

There file past, then, in the song of the soloist the grand gestures of the love of God: the creation with the phantasmagoria of the earth, the waters, the stars, day and night; the exodus from Egypt, sign of liberation and hope for a people; the experience of the desert under the guidance of a shepherd who protects his people from every natural and historical nightmare; and finally there appears on the horizon the land of freedom, where the feet of the worshipers now rest and towards the skies of which they raise their plea. This whole rosary of salvific divine actions is an expression of the *hesed* of the Lord, of his love, punctuated by the liturgical assembly that intones the antiphon, "His love is forever."

Cassiodorus, a Christian author of the sixth century, commented: "The merciful goodness of God shines in every verse of this Psalm like so many stars." The *hesed* of God is "forever"; in humanity, unfortunately, it is fragile, and it is for this reason that the Psalter frequently unfolds on two levels, as we will have occasion to see: divine faithfulness and human unfaithfulness, so as to create an antithetical couplet, as is done in two parallel but opposite Psalms, 105, a canticle of the wonders worked by the Lord, and 106, a confession in a negative vein of the faults that have marred this divine tapestry, faults perpetrated by a people endowed, as it were, with the "genius of unfaithfulness," as observed by one commentator, Andrew Bruce Davidson.

The epiphany of God in history contains, then, a twofold spiritual appeal. The first is an invitation to consider the Lord as an ally, a powerful and loving traveling companion: the invocations of the Psalter are dominated by personal pronouns and possessive adjectives, so much so that the "my/our" addressed to God resounds seventy-five times, while roughly fifty times Israel is called "his people," ten times "his inheritance," and seven times "his flock." There is, therefore, a personal relationship with a God who is indeed "other" with respect to us in his transcendence but is not the cold Unmoved Mover of the Aristotelian tradition; he is not an apathetic and impassible God like an emperor; he is a person who can say "I AM" and who sends Moses to save his people;

his ear hears the cry of the Hebrew slaves, his eyes see the oppressions perpetrated by the Egyptians, his mind knows the sufferings of a people (Ex 3:7–10).

The second appeal that the God of history issues to us is that of trust. We are not at the mercy of an imponderable fate, events are not the result of chaotic fluctuation, the great powers are not the sole and invincible arbiters of human affairs. History—although it is also entrusted to human freedom, which is often disordered and devastating, unfaithful and sinful—bears within itself the design of a transcendent plan of justice and peace that will see as its protagonist that Messiah whom we will meet later. Trust is a fountain of hope. The French poet Charles Péguy, who in 1911 dedicated to this second theological virtue an entire poem, *The portico of the mystery of the second virtue*, which cautioned us: "It is to hope that is the more difficult thing / ashamedly and in a low voice / And the easy thing is to despair / and this is the great temptation." This "younger sister" of faith and charity takes the two older sisters by the hand and pulls them forward along the journey of life, and us with them. The bulb of hope continues to survive, even if it is under the ruins of a difficult and disastrous life, as long as a tiny opening is left.

Dum anima est, spes est, "as long as there is life, there is hope," Cicero wrote to Atticus. But in reality there are persons who are alive and healthy but who have fallen into despair without any desire to get out. So the Marxist philosopher Ernst Bloch, author of the monumental *The Hope Principle* (1954–1959) was correct when he changed the Ciceronian proverb to "As long as there is faith, there is hope." Religion, in fact, places us at a higher level of meaning, it propels us toward a destination of redemption and salvation, it sustains us in the "already but not yet," and through Christianity it shows us in Jesus Christ the face and hand of a God who walks side by side with us down the paths of history, making shine for us the dawn of the resurrection and the future city, that of the heavenly Jerusalem. "Hope . . . is a sure expectation / of the future glory," Dante declares in the *Paradiso* (XXV, 67–68). "The souls of the righteous are in the hand of God . . . For though in the sight of men they are punished, their hope is full of immortality" (Wis 3:1, 4).

So let us live with intensity and trust in the present, because it is already illuminated by the eternity of God who advances with us along the paths of history. Saint Paul admonished: "We do not wish that you should continue to afflict yourselves as do those who have no hope" (1 Thess 4:13). In fact, the well-known spiritual author Thomas Merton wrote that time can flow and slip away through our hands like sand or like seed, it can be arid and dusty or fecund and fruitful. In his encyclical *Spe Salvi*, Benedict XVI delineates in a very evocative way the ultimate estuary of the river of time: "Eternity is not an unending succession of days in the calendar, but something more like the supreme moment of satisfaction, in which totality embraces us and we embrace totality— this we can only attempt. It would be like plunging into the ocean of infinite love, a moment in which time—the before and after—no longer exists."

Let us conclude this brief reflection on the theophany in history by returning to the temple to intone a last prayerful song to the God who is our steadfast ally. It is a mini-hymn, the briefest of all the Psalms, 117, made up of only seventeen Hebrew words, only nine of which are substantial. Perhaps we could follow it by listening to the stupendous rendition that Mozart made of it in 1780 in the *Laudate Dominum* in F major of the *Vesperae solennes de confessore* (K 339). The heart of this, which is a simple ejaculation, a sort of *Gloria Patri* to be appended to the Psalms, lies entirely in the two virtues of the covenant, *hesed*, the "love" that punctuated the "Great Hallel," and *'emet*, the "truth" that is loyalty, faithfulness, the joyful adherence of God to us and of us to him. "Praise the Lord, all nations! Extol him, all peoples! For great is his steadfast love (*hesed*) toward us; and the faithfulness (*'emet*) of the Lord endures for ever."

CHAPTER VI

THE "TRULY NECESSARY" GOD

The Messiah of God

"Today we are sitting, on Christmas Eve, we miserable people, in a frozen room, the wind is howling outside, the wind enters. Come, good Lord Jesus, among us, turn your gaze: because you are truly necessary to us." We will be surprised to hear the name of the author of these verses: it is the famous German dramatist Bertolt Brecht, the proponent of an irreligious vision of existence. And yet this picture that he paints in the collection of his poetry that runs from 1918 to 1933 nearly illustrates in an incisive way the Christological motto of St. Paul: "Though he was rich, yet for your sake he became poor, so that by his poverty you might become rich" (2 Cor 8:9, RSV). The "truly necessary" God is the one who descends among us and becomes one of us.

Well then, our textual and spiritual journey through the Psalter, which has already marked several stages dedicated to the various epiphanies of the face of God, in the Word, in the cosmos, in the temple, in history, now comes before its Messiah, who is the highest expression of his manifestation to humanity. A humanity that Isaiah, in one of his famous messianic hymns, embodies in a miserable vagabond, similar to the indigent family depicted by Brecht: "He will pass through the land, greatly distressed and hungry; and when he is hungry, and will be enraged and will curse his king and his God, and turn this face upward; and will look to the earth, but behold, distress and darkness, the gloom of anguish; and thick darkness. . . . The people who walked in darkness have seen a great light; those who dwelt in a land of deep darkness, on them has light shined. . . ." (Is 8:21–23, 9:2).

It is the divine light that shines upon suffering humanity and envelops the figure of Emmanuel, the messianic king sung of by Isaiah. The Psalms also celebrate with ardor this luminous anticipation that has its heart in the famous oracle addressed to David by the prophet Nathan (2 Sam 7). To the desire of the sovereign to erect a *bajit*, a "house," meaning a temple, for God, so as to have him as a citizen of his kingdom, God opposes a surprising decision: it will be he who will build a *bajit*, a living "house" for the king, or his "household," the descendants from among whom the Messiah will come. Psalm 89 echoes this promise: "Once for all I have sworn by my holiness; I will certainly not lie to David. His line shall endure for ever, his throne before me as long as the sun. It will be established for ever like the moon which is a faithful witness to the skies" (vv. 35–37).

To this figure called "Messiah," meaning "anointed," the Jewish and Christian traditions have applied the whole extensive series of royal songs present in the Psalter, taking literally the emphatic and laudatory aspect, the *Hofstil*, meaning the style of the court. The Messiah is thus the fullness of the expectation of the people of God. We will now pause to contemplate the face of the Messiah thus conceived, the complete reflection of the divine face, ready in the end to welcome its ultimate and supreme New Testament identification in Jesus Christ. There are three features of the Messiah that we will depict, drawing from the text of the Psalms. We will illustrate them by referring to a triptych of messianic hymns that we will not be able to examine in detail, but only evoke in their thematic core.

Let us begin, then, with the scene of the miserable family from the opening words of this chapter. The longing of those poor people is for a new order of justice in society. This is the constant expectation of the people with regard to politics, an expectation that is usually frustrated. Every king who appeared upon the stage of Israel was accompanied by this hope, and the prophets, like Elijah, Amos, Isaiah, or Jeremiah, pointed their fingers against the prevarication of power that disappointed every aspiration to justice. This is why the anticipation was focused on the Messiah, and it is Psalm 72 that interprets this in such impassioned tones that one theologian, Heinz Schürmann (1922–2010), spoke of this song as a "biblical prelude of the *Adveniat regnum tuum* of the Our Father." It is nonetheless significant that the first word of the Psalm is *'elohîm*, "God": the Messiah follows the path of God, who is the Lord of morality.

The invocation takes up almost as a refrain the word "justice": "Give the king thy judgments, to the King's son thy justice! May he judge thy people according to the law, and thy poor with justice! Let the mountains bring peace to the people, and the hills justice! May he render justice to the poor of the people, give deliverance to the needy, and crush the oppressor! . . . For he truly delivers the needy when he calls, the poor and him who has no helper. May he have pity on the weak and the needy, and save the lives of the needy. From oppression and violence he redeems their life; and precious will be their blood in his sight. . . ." (vv. 1–4 12–14). God, in fact, is the *go'el*, the advocate and defender of the defenseless, he is "father of the fatherless and protector of widows" (Ps 68:5, RSV), and his Messiah must imitate him, fighting the injustice and corruption that, as the ancient Romans said, trap in the net of power the gnats, but allow the hornets to sting.

A second feature is visible in a Psalm whose meaning is obscure but has become famous as a Christian messianic song, especially in the liturgy: it is number 110, the *Dixit Dominum*, which has become a part of vespers and has often been used for wonderful musical compositions, as in the *Vespro della Beata Vergine* by Monteverdi. It is based on two oracles, the first a royal one of enthronement (the Lord in fact says to him: "Sit on my right"), while the second is priestly, and it is on this latter that we will dwell: "You are a priest for ever after the order of Melchizedek" (v. 4, RSV). This is an important reference to the priest-king of Genesis (14:17–20) who blesses Abram, the father of all Israel. Of course, David was of the tribe of Judah, and therefore was not able to become a Levitical priest. So in the Messiah king there is a glimpse of another profile of a sacred nature: he will have the function of reminding us of God as "pontiff," extending a bridge between history and the Eternal, through a new and unprecedented priesthood, that of Melchizedek.

The third and last feature is in a divine oracle that has made Psalm 2 famous: "You are my son" is said to the messianic king, "today I have begotten you" (v. 7, RSV). In itself the decree, which scholars call "the royal protocol," had an actual value only in the immanentistic vision of Egypt, in which the Pharaoh was truly the son of the divinity, who—as stated in the "protocol" of Thutmose III (15th century B.C.)—declares: "I am your father, as god I have begotten you to be king upon my throne." In Israel such a conception was unacceptable for monotheism and incompatible with the divine transcendence. Thus the Messiah would have a close connection with the Lord, he would be a member of his family but only by acceptance, he would be son by adoption and certainly not the seed of God in a natural generation.

Just man, priest, and son of God: these are the three aspects of the messianic figure who is at the center of our Psalmic meditation. But precisely because prayer gradually unveils faith and its contents, the three Psalms (72, 110, and 2) enter within the Christian theological and liturgical tradition, where they receive a new interpretation. In fact, the New Testament intuits in these pages, almost as in a cinematic crossfade, the face of Christ, the epitome of the "Anointed One." In him the trilogy of the

qualities that we have described reach their complete ful-
fillment. To use an evocative expression of Benedict XVI
in his work *Jesus of Nazareth: The Infancy Narratives*,
the words of the Psalms are "words in waiting": they are
waiting, that is, to unveil all of their reality, to show their
fullness and perfection.

Thus Jesus is the Just One par excellence, as Peter
would say in his second discourse of Pentecost: "You
denied the Holy and Righteous One" (Acts 3:14, RSV); it
is he who declares "blessed are those who are persecuted
for righteousness' sake" (Mt 5:10, RSV); who descends
from the throne of his glory to become a refugee and
impoverished his whole life, beginning with his very
birth (Psalm 72 is used precisely in the Christmas liturgical period), not possessing during his earthly life even
a stone to use as a pillow, to arrive in the end at the most
infamous form of death, that of crucifixion. A paradox-
ical royalty, then, that "is not of this world," as he would
declare to Pilate and that includes the abandonment of
the dignity that belongs to him: "though he was in the
form of God, [Jesus] did not count equality with God a
thing to be grasped, but emptied himself, taking the form
of a servant, being born in the likeness of men" (Phil 2:6–
7, RSV).

Now let us move on to the second trait. The Letter to
the Hebrews celebrates Christ as "a priest according to
the order of Melchizedek," referring to Psalm 110, and
demonstrates the radical newness of this priesthood. It is
different from Levitical priesthood—"If [Jesus] were on
earth, he would not be a priest at all. . . . having originated

from the tribe of Judah, regarding whom Moses said nothing about priests" (Heb 8:4; 7:14)—and is superior to it, because Melchizedek blessed Abram and in him Levi, a descendant of Abram, thus revealing his primacy with respect to the Hebrew patriarchs themselves. But above all Christ is simultaneously priest, victim, and temple: "he has no need, like the high priests, to offer sacrifices daily . . . he did this once for all" (Heb 7:27, RSV; cf. 9:25–28; 10:11–14). And this was precisely "the high priest that we needed: holy, innocent, without stain, separated from sinners and elevated above the heavens" (7:26).

Finally we come to the third aspect. Christ is Son of God in truth, and not by metaphor. The oracle of Psalm 2:7 thus takes on an unprecedented tonality, which is made clear by the New Testament in its repeated references to this passage above all in a Paschal vein, because it is in the resurrection that the divinity of Christ is fully revealed. Let us simply select the voice of St. Paul in his preaching in Antioch of Pisidia: "We bring you the good news that what God promised to the fathers, this he has fulfilled, for God has accomplished for us, their children by raising Jesus; as also it is written in the second psalm, 'Thou art my Son, today I have begotten thee'" (Acts 13:32–33). It is in this light that we can understand the interesting definition of the Psalter made by Saint Jerome: "It is the lyre that sings of Christ." Those ancient biblical songs are by their nature open to a higher and more perfect dimension.

Before us there shines, therefore, the face of the Messiah, the Christ of God. As the seal of our contemplation of that face, which is the epiphany of the God who is just, holy, and rich in love, let us entrust ourselves to two testimonies addressed precisely to Christ. The first is striking, in spite of its reservation, because it comes from a Jew, the great Franz Kafka (1883–1924), who when asked about Jesus by his friend Gustav Janouch, replied, "He is an abyss of light. One must close one's eyes to keep from falling in." In reality this luminous abyss does not blind, but illuminates and warms if we come to it.

The other testimony is, on the other hand, from a great Christian, Blaise Pascal. As is well known, from the age of thirty-one until his precocious death— in 1662, at the age of thirty-nine—he kept in his doublet a sheet of paper with a memorial that he had entitled *Fire*. Although it is known, let us listen to it again as a testimony of an authentic biblical faith and as a profession of pure and genuine love: "God of Abraham, God of Isaac, God of Jacob, not of the philosophers and of the scholars. Certitude, certitude. Sentiment, joy, peace. God of Jesus Christ. My God and your God. Your God shall be my God. Forgetfulness of the world and everything apart from God. He cannot be found except by the ways indicated by the Gospel."

CHAPTER VII

"EVEN MY EMBRYO YOUR EYES HAVE SEEN!"

God in Man

"In the moment in which I was able to take into my arms my son, I felt a distant reflection of that ineffable and sublime beatitude which must have filled the Creator on the sixth day, when he saw his imperfect yet completed work." These are the words of the main character of *The Emperor's Tomb* (1938), a novel by the Austrian Joseph Roth, a Jewish writer who nonetheless had declared his admiration for St. Therese of Lisieux in his *The Legend of the Holy Drinker*. "Many are the things that are wonderful, but none is more wonderful than man!" exclaimed the chorus of *Antigone* by Sophocles, almost echoing the cry of astonishment of the Psalmist: "I give you thanks because you have made me a stupendous marvel!" (Ps 139:14). The human creature is a wonder, placed at the summit of creation in the narrative of Genesis (1:26–31).

This is, then, the last theophany that we would like to place in our exhibition of Psalmic icons of God. After the epiphanies in the Word, in the cosmos, in the temple and its liturgy, in salvation history and in the Messiah, God appears in the creature *tôb meʾod*, "very beautiful/very good" (Gen 1:31), the glorious divine reflection: man and woman. It is not for reasons of political correctness that we introduce the couple, but we do so on a biblical theological basis. In fact, right from the *incipit* of Genesis a capital anthropological declaration, structured on a rigorous parallelism, presents man and woman as *selem* in Hebrew, *eikôn* in the ancient Greek version, "image" of God: "God created man in his image, in the image of God he created him; male and female he created them" (Gen 1:27, RSV).

Of course, God is not sexually differentiated, as was the case in the indigenous religions of Canaan, the land promised to Israel: this assigned to the prince-god of the pantheon a consort goddess, the principle of naturalistic fertility. For the Bible, instead, the figure of God as Creator has His living and effective symbolic representation precisely in the two who generate, and thus offer the living fabric of salvation history (it is not for nothing that the Priestly Tradition, one of the narrative sources of Genesis, structures its history on the basis of genealogies). The love of man and woman, capable of generating life, is a sign that refers back to God; in the sexually bipolar human creature one has the true living statue of the Creator, such that Israel would not need divine images and idols as the first commandment admonishes (Ex 20:4). This is why it is not rare in the Psalter for the Lord to appear as father and mother at the same time, this being an evocative analogical means of revealing himself in his mystery of love.

The worshiper calls himself, then, "son of thy handmaid" (Ps 86:16, RSV), a juridical formula that designates the one who is born to a specific family clan, in this case that of God. The Psalmist goes even further and confesses: "My father and my mother have forsaken me, but the Lord has taken me up" (27:10). In fact, it is God who is "the father of the orphans" (68:5), and "as a father is tender toward his children, so the Lord is tender toward those who fear him" (103:13). Even the young raven, when he is hungry, chirps at God (147:9), thus recognizing that God is the head of that household which is the entire world. But maternal features also appear in God, so much so that the Hebrew root of the "visceral" love of the mother is applied to God twenty-one times in the Psalter. And the delicious little picture of Psalm 131, which we will look at later, with the believer who represents himself before God like a child in his mother's arms, is almost the perfect depiction. The worshiper knows that the Lord "sees suffering and trouble, he looks at it to take it into his hands," tender and impassioned (10:14).

Now let us meditate on this special divine epiphany which is the living man, selecting two Psalms of great poetic power. Every human creature holds within himself his greatness, although in the diversity of personal identities and in the absolute unrepeatability of each person. The ancient Jewish tradition used a curious comparison: "Men, using one mold, mint many coins that are identical to each other. The King of kings, the Holy and Blessed, has minted the form of each man with the mold of Adam. Nonetheless, you will not find any individual like another. So everyone must say, 'The world has been created for me.'" This nobility of every human person in identity and in diversity begins at his very conception.

Let us listen, then, to one stanza of the first text, Psalm 139: "For thou didst create my inward parts, thou didst knit me together in my mother's womb. I thank thee, for thou hast made me a wonderful marvel. Wonderful are thy works! And my soul recognizes them fully; my frame was not hidden from thee, when I was being made in secret, intricately wrought in the depths of the earth. And thy eyes beheld my unformed substance and in thy book were written, every one of them, the days that were formed for me, when as yet none of them existed. How precious to me are thy thoughts, O God! How complex their substance!" (vv. 13–17). The symbols used by the poet are those—classics in the Bible—of the potter or sculptor and of the weaver, who carefully shape or fashion their masterpiece.

But extraordinarily original is the idea of the gaze of God the creator that passes through the dark and fruitful womb of the mother: this is a miniature of the womb of Mother Earth, but above all it is the workshop of our physical and spiritual future. So then, the divine gaze is directed straight at that wonder which is the *golmî*, a hapax term that occurs only once in the Bible (at least in this form) and designates something rolled up and cylindrical that can be rendered with our term "embryo." With a stirring beat of the wings the Psalmist proclaims that, while he was still so tiny and shapeless, God already intuited the whole expanse of days, thoughts, works that this little creature would later live and realize in his future history. One is spontaneously led to set side-by-side the divine declaration that we encounter in Jeremiah, in the Servant of the Lord, in the Baptist, and in Saint Paul: "Before I formed you in the mother's womb I knew you, and before you were born I consecrated you" (Jer 1:5; cf. Is 49:1,5; Luke 1:15–17; Gal 1:15). A transcendent knowledge that Psalm 139 celebrates in the preceding stanzas, extolling in exhilarating verses the divine omniscience (vv. 1–6) and omnipresence (vv. 7–12), according to which the human creature is always before the eyes of the Lord and always accompanied by his hand.

Let us seek, therefore, the divine presence in every human creature from the point of his primordial genesis; but let us also discover the constant attention with which God accompanies man in his history without ever leaving him alone. The human creature is the place in which to intercept God, in part because his own Son has walked the entire journey of conception, gestation, birth, growth, and death, he too becoming human *sarx*, "flesh," with a beginning and an end.

The amazement in the face of such a complex and wonderful child, in spite of his simplicity, expands to the complete man in his maturity, who stands above the other creatures. This is the second Psalmic text that invites us to this contemplation: a famous hymn, Psalm 8, which in

1969 Paul VI entrusted to the American astronauts Neil
Armstrong and Buzz Aldrin so that they might place it
on the surface of the moon with these words: "Man is
at the center of this enterprise, and in it he is revealed
simultaneously as giant and divine, not in himself, but
in his beginning and in his destiny. Honor, then, to man,
honor to his dignity, to his spirit, to his life!"

The sacred poet is immersed in a starry night: "I look
at thy heavens, the work of thy fingers, the moon and the
stars which thou hast established" (v. 3, RSV). A question
arises spontaneously: "What is man that thou art mindful
of him, and the son of man that thou dost care for him?"
(v. 4, RSV). The answer seems to be a given and speaks of
nothingness, of disproportion with respect, of course, to
the spatial immensity of the sky and the grandiose solar
system. But the imbalance is above all with regard to the
Creator: in fact, the heavens are "yours" and the moon and
the stars have been set in the firmament by "your fingers."
This last locution is very refined with respect to the traditional one, "the work of your hands": the gigantic galaxies
and the constellations God has created with the delicacy
of embroidery or chisel work, with the refinement of the
artist who runs his fingers along the strings of a harp.

The first reaction is therefore one of dismay: how can
God "be mindful" and "care for" this creature, so fragile
and microscopic, this "reed, the most fragile thing in all
of nature . . . against which it is not necessary that the
whole universe should arm itself to annihilate it because
a vapor, a drop of water is enough to kill it" (Pascal)?

But then comes the great surprise that dominates the

rest of Psalm 8 (vv. 5–9): this fragile creature has within him a dignity so great as to make him "little less than a god," because he is "crowned" by the Creator with a royal diadem. Man is, in fact, the lieutenant of the Lord himself in the dominion of being: "Thou hast put all things under his feet, all sheep and oxen, and also the beasts of the field, the birds of the air, and the fish of the sea, whatever passes along the paths of the sea." That "all" is arresting, insistent in its repetition, indicating a full and complete authority. It is not, however, a power acquired autonomously or by *hybris*, meaning through conquest in a fight against God, as takes place in the Greek myth of Prometheus and of the fire stolen from the gods, nor is it a dominion obtained solely through human intelligence and effort, as the humanism of the Renaissance and the Enlightenment would suggest.

It is a power delegated by the only one who can call the universe "the work of his hands/fingers," the Lord. To our weak and often selfish hands is entrusted the entire spectrum of creatures so that we may care for them and shape them, understand and transform them. The hymn is, therefore once again, the celebration of the divine traits that are faintly concealed in the human creature, who is invited to develop his knowledge, his work, his care for creation.

Unfortunately man often reveals himself as a tyrant who devastates the earth, lording himself over it, deforming its basic laws and structures. This is why that splendid homily or treatise which is the Letter to the Hebrews applied the Psalm to the perfect man, to Christ "crowned with glory and honor because of the death that he suffered for the sake of all" (cf. Heb 2:6–9). The nocturnal atmosphere of the Psalm can therefore blend into the night of Christmas when Jesus makes his entrance to build the kingdom of justice, peace, and harmony.

Let us take our leave of this last divine epiphany, the one closest to us. It is the manifestation of God who accompanies his creatures with tenderness and respect, with delicacy and love, as we are reminded by the Psalm of the twelve "most beautiful names" of the Lord, different from the ninety-nine "most beautiful names" of Allah in the Muslim tradition. In Psalm 146, in fact, there are no abstract or transcendent titles, as is the case in Islam, but rather there are concrete, historical, existential titles. Let us sing them like a litany addressed to God the creator, father, and savior, but also as our commitment to protect the dignity of every human person, becoming imitators of God the Father and Lord of all, "who desires all men to be saved and to come to the knowledge of the truth" (1 Tim 2:4, RSV).

Here is the "litany" in honor of God in Psalm 146: "The Lord has made the heavens and the earth, the sea and all that is in them, he keeps the faith for ever, he executes justice for the oppressed; he gives food to the hungry. The Lord sets the prisoners free; the Lord opens the eyes of the blind. The Lord lifts up those who are bowed down; the Lord loves the righteous. The Lord watches over the sojourners, he upholds the widow and the fatherless; but the way of the wicked he brings to ruin. The Lord will reign for ever, thy God, O Zion, to all generations. Praise the Lord!" (vv. 6–10).

PART TWO

THE FACE OF MAN

I have been accustomed to call this book, I think
not inappropriately, "An Anatomy of all the Parts
of the Soul;" for there is not an emotion of which
any one can be conscious that is not here represented as in a mirror. Or rather, the Holy Spirit
has here drawn to the life all the griefs, sorrows,
fears, doubts, hopes, cares, perplexities, in short,
all the distracting emotions with which the minds
of men are wont to be agitated.

—John Calvin,
Commentary on the Psalms
(1557)

CHAPTER VIII

"LIKE A WEANED CHILD"

The Believing Man

Pierre Prigent, in his commentary on Revelation (1980), notes that there is a verse of such beauty and incisiveness as to make fall from the hands of the exegetes the sophisticated instruments of their analysis to leave room for the purity of the text. It is a little portrait set as a seal of that last of the seven letters that open that biblical book, addressed to a church of Asia Minor, that of Laodicea. It seems to be a portrait of many contemporary Christian communities, and also of the very society in which we are immersed. In fact, it hoists the gray banner of lukewarmness, of superficiality, of mediocrity, of banality, far from both the flaming ardor of goodness and love and from the tragic awareness of the chill of evil. It is not immoral, but amoral. And thus Christ's finger is pointed in ferocious accusation: "I know your works: you are neither cold nor hot. Would that you were cold or hot! So, because you are lukewarm, and neither cold nor hot, I will spew you out of my mouth" (Rev 3:15–16, RSV).

But at the end of the letter, this nausea seems to dissolve and there appears the scene to which we made reference: "I stand at the door and knock; if any one hears my voice and opens the door, I will come in to him and eat with him, and he with me" (Rev 3:20, RSV). Christ, then, passes through the streets of the world, "your feet still bleed on our pavement," sang the French poet Pierre Emmanuel. He comes to the door and knocks: this sequence contains a connotation that can escape notice. In fact, it refers back to the amorous symbolism of the lover who stands at the door of the beloved, who shows herself hesitant to open. The popular poetical form of the song sung beneath the window of the woman desired is a literary device known to the Greek world as the *paraklausithyron*, "standing outside the closed door." It is a descriptive feature of the Song of Songs when twice the beloved "stands behind our wall, gazing in at the windows, looking through the lattice" (Song 2:9, RSV), and then in the middle of the night he "is knocking. 'Open to me, my sister . . . he puts his hand to the latch" of the door (Song 5:2, 4).

The scene, then, outside of the metaphor, celebrates in the first place the primacy of grace, the *cháris* that becomes caritas, as we have already seen at the beginning of our journey. If Christ did not pass by and knock, we would remain closed up in our solitary and autonomous history. We thus have nearly a summary of the series of Psalmic theophanies examined so far. But a new element makes its entrance. It is up to us to listen to that knocking and to that voice that calls. It is up to the one who is closed off in his space and time to throw open the door.

This is the moment of human freedom, of *pístis*, the faith that accepts *cháris*, the call, the gift, the theophany. There are some who choose not to be disturbed or distracted by the noise, by the chatter, by the high volume of sound, by laziness or indifference, remain seated and ignore that voice, like the woman in the Song of Solomon who makes excuses not to get up and open the door for her beloved.

But for those who have grasped the handle of the door and opened it, what a surprise: it is he, the Lord! Then, just like Abraham who hastened to welcome the three mysterious guests, preparing a sumptuous feast and receiving the gift of the life of Isaac (Gen 18), so also that family which has welcomed Christ has him as a guest at table. And the meal is a preeminent sign of communion, of sharing, of intimacy. This is the beginning of the new life, the *dikaiosyne*, the Pauline "justification" that gives rise to the new creature. It is the embrace between the two loves, divine *caritas* and the amorous trust of the believer. It is precisely from this encounter that we will now begin the second part of our journey. If so far the protagonist has been God who has knocked and has presented himself with his Word, his action in the world, in the temple, in history, in his Messiah, and in the heart of man, the focus now shifts to the human creature who responds to his God with his Word, his works, his unique identity, his finiteness and culpability, his expectations and hopes.

If on the previous stages we have been on pilgrimage around the sources of the Jordan and the Sea of Tiberias, the theater of the works and days of Jesus Christ, of his first unveiling, now—to continue with the same metaphor—we will navigate along the course of that river, a serpentine course that is extremely complex. In fact, in order to travel sixty-five miles as the crow flies, the Jordan meanders over two hundred miles of terrain, becoming an emblem of human life—rambling, scattered, tumultuous. Nonetheless, what sustains us on this journey—which we will describe step-by-step in the following meditations— is trust, what the theologians call *fides qua*, meeting the faith by which we adhere to that God whom we have come to know in *fides quae*, or the content of the truths discovered by contemplating the divine face, as we have previously done. So then, one of the most intense literary genres of the Psalms is precisely that of the "Psalms of trust": in them resounds "the voice of the bride addressed to her bridegroom," as the Second Vatican Council says (*Sacrosanctum Concilium*, no. 84), after the Bridegroom has spoken to us. As Saint Jerome reminds us, "Do you pray? That is you talking to the Bridegroom. Do you read? It is he who speaks to you" (*Epistula* 22:25).

Let us entrust the portrait of the faithful and trust-ing worshiper who remains united with his God—amid laughter and tears, light and darkness, life and death—to a delicious and tender hymn made up of only about thirty words in the original Hebrew, only about fifteen of which are indispensable. Psalm 131 has at its center almost a cameo: a mother and her child serenely united to her. The symbolism of spiritual childhood is a classic in mystical theology: we need think only of Saint Therese of Lisieux (1873–1897) and of her *Story of a Soul*, with the extolling of the "little way," of "remaining small," of "being in the arms of Jesus," or of our invocation of a spiritual master, Léonce de Grandmaison: "Holy Mother of God, preserve in me the heart of a child, pure and clear like a stream!" The fact that spiritual childhood is not a sweet and sentimental childishness appears in the very structure of the Psalm, which is divided into two sections.

The first, in a negative form, describes the antithesis of spiritual trust: "My heart is not lifted up, my eyes are not raised with pride; I do not go towards things too great and too marvelous for me" (v. 1). In Hebrew there are "vertical" images according to which the person raises himself up almost as a sign of challenge: the "lifting up" of the heart is *gabah*, a verb that refers to summits, to the mountain; the "raising up" of the eyes is *rûm*, a raising oneself up to look down with arrogance and disdain; while the *halak*, the "path," ascends toward the peaks of stunning power and success.

This is the polar opposite of faith, the arrogance that deceives man into placing himself in the same position as God: this is the "original" sin of "[being] like God, knowers of good and evil" (Gen 3:4). One immediately thinks of this stupendous satirical elegy of Isaiah, in which the king of Babel proclaims with arrogance: "I will ascend to heaven; above the stars of God I will raise my throne; I will dwell on the mount of assembly in the real divine dwelling; I will ascend above the heights of the clouds, I will make myself equal to the Most High" (Is 14:13–14).

This agitated, fanatical, turbulent picture is replaced with the positive scene in which emerges the face of the true believer. The atmosphere is hushed and silent, as the worshiper murmurs: "I instead have calmed and quieted my soul, like a child weaned in the arms of its mother; like a child that is weaned is my soul" (v. 2). One should note the repetition, typical of the "Psalms of ascent" to which our text belongs, which seems to soften and prolong the quiet and peace of that stanza in which a child is embraced by his mother. Also important here are the "horizontal" images the soul is "stretched out" like a plain, and it is "tranquil," which in Hebrew is *dmm*, a word that denotes profound silence. But it is relevant to fix one's gaze on that child who is often conceived as a tranquil and satiated newborn after sucking the milk from the breast of his mother.

In reality, the Hebrew word is *gamûl*, and it designates the "weaned child," carried on the shoulders according to Eastern custom. Now, the official age of weaning was advanced in that society, occurring around the age of three and marked with a big celebration of the family clan. The child, then, is connected to his mother by a more personal and intimate relationship, intentional and not merely stimulated by the physical instinct for food. Authentic trust is therefore not blind abandonment: it is adherence with one's freedom and personality, as in the writings of Saint Elizabeth of the Trinity, another mystical figure of great intensity, who lived only to the age of twenty-six: "God has placed in my heart an infinite thirst and a tremendous need to love that only he can satisfy. So I go to him as the child goes to his mother, so that he may fill and permeate all and take me in his arms." This bond is sometimes awkward and hesitating because, as the Lord confesses in a tender soliloquy in the pages of the prophet-father Hosea:

"When Israel was a child, I loved him . . . I led them with cords of compassion, with the bands of love, and I became to them as one who eases the yoke on their jaws, and I bent down to them and fed them" (Hos 11:1, 4, RSV).

In a time like our own, which has lost the taste for refinement and tenderness, for the simplicity and limpidity of the soul, it is necessary to rediscover "being children" not out of affectation or sentimentalism, but in the footsteps of the admonition of Jesus to "become like children in order to enter the kingdom of heaven" (cf. Mt 18:1–5). As is well known, Jesus himself prays in this way: "I bless thee, Father, Lord of heaven and earth, that thou hast hidden these things from the wise and understanding and revealed them to babes" (Mt 11:25). And if we have lost this limpidity of the faith, let us recall what the writer Georges Bernanos (1888–1948) acknowledged about himself in a letter: "I have lost childhood and cannot recover it except through holiness."

Even amid the temptations of pride, amid the tempest of impure tensions, amid the fascination of success and power, we must preserve a foundation of serene trust that will allow us to pray like Blessed John Henry Newman (1801–1890), while the ship on which he was traveling near the Straits of Bonifacio between Sardinia and Corsica was being tossed by a storm: "Lead, Kindly Light, amidst th' encircling gloom, / Lead Thou me on! The night is dark, and I am far from home, / Lead Thou me on! / . . . I do not ask to see / The distant scene; one step enough for me."

CHAPTER IX

"A BREATH IS EVERY MAN"

The Fragile Human Creature

"Lord, the best testimony / that we can give of our dignity / is this ardent sob that rolls from age to age / and dies at the threshold of your eternity." He had gathered all the "flowers of evil" in a dissipated life, but the poet Charles Baudelaire (1821–1867) had the courage to give voice to all of the sufferers and sinners of the earth, issuing this extreme invocation to God, accompanied by an "ardent sob" of sorrow and repentance. This is the cry that is raised repeatedly in the Psalter, which in this way embodies the sigh of sorrow that rises from the earth toward heaven. A sigh that has always found expression in literature, as suggested by the Greek tragedian Aeschylus, who in *The Persians* presented this yearning of the human creature but allowed to fall into the void every response that came from above, from the "secrecy of shadow."

This is an experience that has elicited all forms of theology and has become the substance of endless prayers in all the religions. It is significant to note that almost a third of the Psalter is made up of personal supplications or communal lamentations. It is striking to read the protest addressed to God and formulated in the "Why" that is typical of many invocations racked with pain, or by the fourfold "Till when?" of Psalm 13, rising to a crescendo: "Till when, O Lord, Wilt thou forget me? Forever? Till when wilt thou hide thy face from me? Till when must I feel nightmares in my soul, and have sorrow in my heart ever day? Till when shall my enemy be exalted over me?" (vv. 1–2). Each one of us, when he feels his body and spirit touched by the frozen hand of trial, and of evil, of solitude, of sickness, and of death, raises a sigh, a lamentation, a plea, once again confessing with the Psalmist: "I kept my faith, even when I said, 'I am greatly afflicted'" (Ps 116:10, RSV).

The worshiper in the Psalms therefore gives voice to all of us when we experience what in Hebrew is called *sar*, meaning "distress," a word that indicates a narrowing, a confinement without air, terrible for one who is used to the wide open spaces of life. For this reason, "liberation" (Ps 4:1: "From distress, you have liberated me") evokes the free expanses of the countryside or of the spacious and solitary steppe in which the person can move, run, enjoy, and live in the light. We will therefore seek in these and some other stages of our spiritual pilgrimage to encounter the various faces of suffering, because—as the French writer Michel Tournier wrote—if the day is the same for all, the night is different for each because everyone populates it with his own fears.

Ours will therefore be a selection of experiences on which we will reflect in order to entrust to God every sorrow and expectation. One premise is indispensable. Suffering and evil are connected to the very identity of creaturehood, which is limited and fallen; as John Paul II wrote in *Salvifici Doloris*, it is "essential to the nature of man . . . almost inseparable from man's earthly existence." Sickness, for example, is not only a physiological, biological, and medical question, but is also an existential, philosophical, psychological, and theological question. This is why the American writer Susan Sontag, when she was struck with cancer, recounted her experience in 1978 in a book that was significantly entitled *Illness As Metaphor*. At this sickbed of the suffering person, medical science is not enough, but "compassion" is also necessary; treatment cannot ignore humanity, corporal anatomy demands attention to spirituality (even at the neutral and "secular" level there is interest in the therapeutic effect of prayer in illness).

The Psalms record again and again this deep anthropological root of suffering. An excellent example of this is Psalm 39, "perhaps the most beautiful of all the Psalmic elegies," as the exegete Heinrich Ewald wrote. It is an intense and bitter meditation on the "evil of living," on the limitation of being a creature, on the misery of the human condition, on the radical fragility of existence. The poet ties together the whole experience of "how fragile I am" (v. 5) with a word dear to Qoheleth, who uses it no fewer than thirty-eight times: *hebel*, "breath, void, vanity." Here it is reiterated three times: "Surely every man stands as a mere breath! Surely like a shadow is man that passes! Surely like a breath he turmoils . . . surely

every man is a mere breath!" (vv. 5–6, 11). Also powerful
is the image—which would be adopted by Shakespeare
in *Macbeth*—of man as a walking shadow, an image that
becomes more biblical as the Psalm continues: "I am thy
passing guest, a pilgrim, like all my fathers" (v. 12), which
would be borrowed by Goethe, for whom "man is a sad
wayfarer on the darkened earth."

This is therefore a meditation on the finiteness of
being a creature, as is clearly stated in the opening of the
song when it describes the inner torment: "I remained
totally dumb and was silent without happiness, and my
distress was exasperated, my heart became hot within
me. As I mused, the fire burned" (vv. 2–3). And finally
the explosion from the lips, which cry out: "Lord, reveal
to me my end, and what is the measure of my days," a
measure made up of "a few handbreadths," because "my
lifetime is as nothing in thy sight" (vv. 4–5). The voice
of Job is the same: "My days are swifter than a weaver's
shuttle, and come to their end without hope. Remember
that my life is a breath; my eyes no longer contemplate
happiness. . . . Let me alone, for my days are a breath"
(Job 7:6–7, 16). Or that of Saint James: "What is your life?
For you are a mist that appears for a little time and then
vanishes" (James 4:14, RSV).

These and other powerful words of the Bible and of
the ascetical tradition are a necessary lashing in an atmosphere as superficial as the one in which contemporary
society is immersed, preoccupied to the utmost with
"heaping up without knowing who will gather" (cf. v. 6).
There is a ferocious representation of this state already in

the *Diary* of Kierkegaard: "The ship is in the hands of the cook, and what the megaphone of the captain transmits is no longer the route but what we will eat tomorrow." The great means of communication, starting with television and the Internet, teach us everything about trends and lifestyles, about food and consumption, but they ignore every question and answer about the meaning of existence.

This is a climate that we all breathe, to which we adapt ourselves and that extinguishes the great questions about the value of life. The Psalmist, on the contrary, forces a bending of the mind toward what we want to ignore, toward our radical misery, toward death. Death is the great refugee of contemporary culture, and yet never has it been so at home in everyday violence, in mayhem, in conflict, in the constant choice of death that is made without ethical reflection or hesitation. The final prayer of the Psalm, however, is striking. It is a poor and bare invocation that also appears on the lips of many simple persons who are tried by life, an invocation that we must respect even in its brutality, precisely because the Word of God has allowed in its pages both the harsh lamentations of many worshipers, and the heartrending cry of Job, and the composed but harsh reaction of Qoheleth.

The worshiper in Psalm 39, in fact, concludes his plea/meditation in this way: "Hear my prayer, O Lord, and give ear to my cry; do not be deaf to my sobs! . . . Look away from me, that I may breathe, before I depart and nothing remains of me" (vv. 12–13). It is evident that the otherworldly horizon is still empty in this conception, as in other pages of the Old Testament. This asks, then, only to "breathe" for a moment, literally to "swallow [my] saliva," the location also in Arabic indicates a moment of reprieve. It is only this that he asks of God: give me a bit of peace before I fall into the abyss of nothingness. Precisely as Job prayed: "Let me alone, that I may truce and a moment of joy before I go on a journey from which I shall not return, to the land of deep darkness and of mortal shadows" (Job 10:20–22).

Evil, suffering, and sin are the epiphanies of the limitation of the human creature. In the following stages we will select only a few traits that in the Psalter are often depicted under monstrous, hunting, or warlike symbols, or personified in the "enemy." Sometimes there also appears an attempt to rationalize and simplify evil through philosophical-theological theorems, like the so-called "theory of retribution," against which Job would react harshly. According to this sort of moral technology, with every spin of the wheel of the pair "crime-punishment" and "justice-reward" the problem of suffering would be resolved, because it would be nothing other than the seal of expiation of an offense. Although it does have some real applications, the idea is refuted by reality itself, and Jesus reiterates this before the man born blind: "It was not that this man sinned, or his parents, but that the works of God might be made manifest in him" (Jn 9:3, RSV). And here appears the power of the revolution introduced by Christ: evil, from being the seat of satanic epiphanies, becomes a place of salvific theophany.

Or else one is still seeking to rediscover a meaning, still by the rational way, considering the trial of suffering as a *paideia*, a pedagogical catharsis that leads to conversion, purification, or interior formation, as Aeschylus affirmed: "wisdom is acquired with suffering," according to which suffering becomes a valuable instrument for breaking through the slumber of the soul, the lethargy of the mind, the obtuseness of the conscience. In fact, one never emerges from a deeply felt trial completely unharmed and the same as before. Our Psalmist also repeats his conviction: "When thou dost chasten man with rebukes for sin" (v. 11, RSV). Of course, an illness can also teach the sense of limitation, debunking every illusion of omnipotence, it can make us recognize the need for the other and his affection, indicate a new hierarchy of values, and create in those who do not believe a tension toward transcendence. Nonetheless, suffering generates at the same time a more profound and radical crisis of meaning that cannot be rationalized or debunked or ignored.

This is why we will continue by seeking in the following stages of our journey other faces of suffering, profiles that can sometimes be seen on the outside in the diseased flesh, in collective tragedies, in solitude, and other times are interior like the silence of God or the confession of sin. Evil, in fact, not only breaks the connection with the world and with one's neighbor (Job, in 19:17, significantly protests that his wife has become disgusted with his breath), but also brings into crisis the relationship with God, so much so that theology arises almost as theodicy, or as the apologetics of God before the looming of evil.

We will now conclude, keeping alive in our hearts the questions of the Psalmist. The saints did this as well with the words of the Psalms. At the beginning of 397, Saint Ambrose, enfeebled by this time, dictated the commentary on Psalm 44, a dramatic national lamentation. Having arrived at verse twenty-four, he wrote: "It is hard to drag for so long a body that is already enfolded in the shadow of death. Rouse thyself! Why sleepest thou, O Lord? Awake! Do not cast us off forever!" These were his last lines: they were also his last prayer, severe and bare like that of Psalm 39, but for the saint implicitly open to a response of light.

CHAPTER X

"I AM EXHAUSTED: HEAL ME!"

Suffering Man

"What sense would all of this make if our little girl were only diseased flesh, a bit of suffering life, and not instead a little white host that surpasses all of us, an immensity of mystery? . . . We must not think of suffering as something that is torn from us, but as something that is given to us and that we give . . . I had the sensation, in approaching your little bed without speaking, that I was approaching an altar . . . We had hoped that Françoise would die. Is that not bourgeois sentimentalism? Who knows, instead, if it is not demanded of us that we keep and adore a host in our midst. My little Françoise, you are for me an image of faith." It is the French philosopher Emmanuel Mounier (1905–1950) who offers us this testimony in the face of his daughter who was struck with an acute encephalitis that had thrown her into a dark night from which she would never emerge.

It is above all the Christian faith— a religion of the "flesh" and of bodies that, with the incarnation of God, have become holy—that has been able to create a spirituality of physical suffering, without canceling out the realism of creatural limitation, but introducing an openness to a higher plane of meaning. Already in the religious search of humanity are felt to vibrate the seeds of this anticipation, as one reads in *Oedipus at Colonus* by Sophocles: "The suffering is so much that it touches man without reason. May God in his justice lead it back on high."

This expectation becomes certainty in the Christian faith, as we will see; but this is also the case in the Psalter before it. We will now select two songs of the suffering person, among the many possible, one of an exhausted sick person and the other of an isolated person, aware that every physical and psychological suffering is—as we have already had occasion to say—a global anthropological experience, an expression of a more radical and intimate evil. And this regardless of the already noted "theory of retribution" that always interprets in a moral key that is psycho-physical, like illness.

Now, the various spectrum of syndromes stretches out over many prayers of the Psalms, from the more traumatic forms like leprosy ("My wounds grow foul and fester . . . my kidneys burn with fever, and there is no soundness in my flesh," Ps 38:5, 7) to the simpler lack of appetite: "I eat ashes like bread, and from my tears pour my drink" (Ps 102:9).

In 1952 a monk and exegete of the abbey of Maredsous, Hilaire Duesberg, published a *Psautier des malades*, collecting all of the pleas of the sick in the Psalter, beginning with Psalm 6, the first to issue a plea from the arid terrain of physical suffering. In the praying patient the bones tremble from fever, tears stream from the eyes, the bed is the place where one spends bitter hours. The nightmare of old age and death appears before the sufferer, as hard as solitude or the malice of former friends.

Here are a few passages of this lament which reveals how realistic, sincere, and free biblical prayer is: "Be gracious to me, O Lord, for I am exhausted; O Lord, heal me, for my bones are trembling and my breathing is troubled. But thou, O Lord—till when? . . . I am weary with my long laments; every night I flood my bed with tears; I drench my couch with my weeping. My eyes waste away because of grief, they grow old because of my afflictions" (Ps 6:2–3, 6–7). Of course, everything is dominated by the theological interpretation of retribution according to which, in suffering, one feels God as an inexorable judge who is striking without pity: "O Lord, do not strike me in your disdain, nor chasten me in thy wrath" (6:1). But what clearly emerges is precisely the "corporeal" paradigm, the sign of a "carnal" prayer.

Three parts of the body are dominant in this self-portrait of the patient. First of all the *nefesh*, the "throat," and therefore the "breath," but also the whole being, since this word—as is well known—also includes the meaning of "soul," the vital principle (v. 3). Then there are the "bones" (v. 2), which indicate the very structure of the physiological being, and therefore if these tremble under the strain of fever, it is as if the whole organism were subjected to a devastating tempest. Finally the "eyes" (vv. 6–7), which become weakened in their ability to see because of the weeping that seems to corrode and transform them into the bleary pupils of an elderly person. This description is accompanied by the hyperbole of the flood of tears that turn the bed of the sick person into a sort of irrigated field.

From this panorama of desolation and ruin, there arises to God a cry of frustration, the typical "Till when . . . ?" (v. 3), an elliptical question, direct in its audacity, addressed to an indifferent God. This is a sincere expression of desperation, but paradoxically also of extreme trust in God, a bit in the much more vehement manner of Job: "I want to incriminate the Almighty! It is against God that I want to protest!" (Job 13:3).

Luther, commenting on the revolt of Job, observes that perhaps God listens with greater attention and without being scandalized even to the blasphemous cry of the desperate sufferer than he does to the commonplace and composed Sunday praises of a comfortable person. The Psalmist is, in any case, certain that the last word of God will not be that of punitive abandonment. And this is why the lamentation gives way at the end to the confidence of being heard: "The Lord has heard my supplication; the Lord accepts my prayer" (v. 9, RSV). It is precisely in this light that the Psalm can become the prayer of all of us when illness in its thousands of variations pervades our bodies and oppresses our souls.

There is, however, along with physical suffering that obscure nightmare which is called "solitude," "the playground of Satan," as it was defined by the writer Vladimir

Nabokov (1899–1977). Of course, there is a valuable sol-itude made up of silence and reflection, a genuine diet of the spirit, but the isolation of a person in an apartment, facing a bare wall, a telephone that never rings, nothing but the remembrance of the dead, with no one left to think of him, touch him, listen to him with tenderness, is a ter-rible curse. This is similar to the experience of the second Psalmist we will now call upon, who was perhaps a priest of Jerusalem sent into exile in the north of the Holy Land, near the Jordan River. This is the cantor of Psalm 42/43, mistakenly divided into two parts but united in its theme and in the very antiphon that is reiterated three times in a musical crescendo: "Why are you cast down, O my soul, and why are you disquieted within me? Hope in God; for I shall again praise him, my help and my God" (42:5,11; 43:5, RSV). This refrain's hymn is marked by the "Why?" of the sufferer: he finds no meaning in his drama (in the Psalm, the "why?" recurs ten times!) It is a refrain evoc-atively established on a psychological dialogue with one's own "ego," one's lacerated conscience.

This poetic and spiritual jewel should resound in our hearts and our ears, against the background of one of the masterpieces of polyphony, the unforgettable *Sicut cervus* by Pierluigi da Palestrina. The plot is three-dimensional. Behind is the past that is gone, evoked with nostalgia as every sufferer does. For the worshiper, it was the joy of the liturgy. He confesses, in fact: "My soul is cast down within me" at the memory of when he used to lead the crowd in procession to the temple "with glad shouts and songs of thanksgiving, a multitude keeping festival" (42:4,

RSV). Because of this allusion, one thinks of a priest as the author of the plea.

Now, instead, he is immersed in a bitter present, in exile in Galilee, at the foot of Mount Hermon, from the cliffs of which arises and flows the Jordan with its cascades (42:6–7). The contrast is strong: the worshiper is surrounded by many waters, but they cannot quench his thirst; the only water that passes over his dry lips is that of tears, and his only thirst is for the water of Zion, where there is the Lord, "the fountain of living waters" (Jer 2:13). A single word (*nefesh*), as we already know, expresses both a spiritual thirst of the soul and the parched throat, which launches a cry similar to the bellowing of the doe at a drought-stricken stream.

But Psalm 43 discloses the third act, projected into the future: in the Missal of Pius V it was the prayer that the priest recited at the foot of the altar. It is the dream-hope in a God whose final sentence is not expulsion, exile, isolation of his faithful. The Lord, in fact, will send two of his messengers: Light and Truth (43:3). They will take the worshiper by the hand, pull him from the gelid curtain of his adversaries who are repeating to him sarcastically "Where is your God" (42:3, 10), and lead him back to the "holy mountain" of Zion. The final destination, now awaited only in trust, will be in the very heart of the temple: "I will go to the altar of God, to God my exceeding joy; and I will praise thee with the lyre, O God, my God" (43:4, RSV). An approach in stages: from far away, the "mountain" of Zion, then the divine "dwelling" of the temple, and finally the "altar" of the ritual sacrifice, where the thirst and yearning for God will be satisfied forever.

None of the supplications of the Psalms, except for one (Ps 88), ever flow into the estuary of desperation, but on their final horizon there always appears a glimmer of light. "God did not come," wrote Paul Claudel, "to explain suffering, he came to fill it with his presence." Decisive in this regard is what we could call the "Christology of suffering." In Christ, God has bent down to human suffering and to evil. Jesus "went about doing good and healing all who were under the power of evil," Peter would say in his proclamation to the centurion Cornelius (Acts 10:38). Emblematic is the relationship of Christ with the lepers, the "excommunicated" sick of civil and religious society: "Moved with pity, he stretched out his hand and touched him, and said to him, 'I will; be clean'" (Mk 1:41, RSV). He takes the evil and impurity upon himself, allowing himself to become infected, in order to liberate and save. Forty-two percent of the account of the public life of Jesus according to the Gospel of Mark is made up of healings: his hands and words privilege suffering and misery.

But the incarnation goes further, because it involves on the part of God in the Son the full assumption of human limitation against every Gnostic and spiritualistic vision. This is the great Pauline "scandal" of the cross (1 Cor 1:23). The account of the Passion of Christ is exemplary precisely because it attests to the passage of Jesus over the entire span of suffering and mortality.

Everything begins with the fear of death, when Jesus is sweating blood beneath the fronds of the olive trees of Gethsemane: "Father, if thou art willing, remove this cup from me" (Lk 22:42, RSV). It continues with the complete experience of the many obscure reflections of suffering: from solitude, with the abandonment and betrayal of his friends, to the physical tortures, from the hatred of the crowd to the silence of the Father, a terrible moment for the Son, from the tragic death by crucifixion ("and Jesus uttered a loud cry, and breathed his last," Mk 15:37, RSV) to becoming a limp cadaver destined for burial. Moreover, Saint Paul will come to the point of affirming that on Christ, the only just man, is placed the enormous weight of human sin: "For our sake he made him to be sin who knew no sin, so that in him we might become the righteousness of God" (2 Cor 5:21, RSV).

But in being martyred and killed there is always concealed the Son, and therefore the divinity. And it is for this reason that in our suffering and dying, through the total solidarity of Christ, the Son of God, a seed of life has been planted, a seed of resurrection, a principle of redemption. The dawn of Easter that unveils this radical transformation of human suffering and death: "Christ has been raised from the dead, the first fruits of those who have fallen asleep" (1 Cor 15:20, RSV). The proclamation contained in the "words in waiting" of Isaiah concerning the messianic Servant of the Lord is fulfilled: "He shall see the fruit of the travail of his soul . . . make many to be accounted righteous" (53:11, RSV). In Christ God does not protect us from all suffering, but in all suffering he upholds us and sets us free.

Let us pray, then, on the day of suffering with the invocation present in an apocryphal book of the New Testament, the Acts of Thomas: "Lord Jesus Christ, companion and hope of the sick, hope and trust of the poor, refuge and repose of the weary, shelter and harbor of those who travel in the region of darkness, you are the physician who heals freely. You have been crucified for all men and for you no one has been crucified! In the land of illness may you be the physician, in the land of weariness may you be the strengthener; O physician of our bodies, give life to our souls, make us your dwelling and may the Holy Spirit abide in us" (no. 156).

CHAPTER XI

CRIME, PUNISHMENT, FORGIVENESS

Man the Sinner

"If you knew your sins, you would lose heart!" says the Lord to my soul, which replies: "If you unveil them to me, I will despair!" The Lord concludes: "No, you will not despair, because your sins will be revealed to you in the very moment they are forgiven you!" This is a presentation in dialogue form of one of the many brilliant *Thoughts* of Pascal (1623–1662). In it is clearly seen that the classical pairing of "crime and punishment"—also illustrated in the famous novel of this name by Dosto-evsky—in genuine biblical spirituality is turned into the trio of "crime, punishment, and forgiveness." This is what we also discover in the Psalter, leafing through the "seven penitential Psalms" (Ps 6, 32, 38, 51, 102, 130, 143): genuine songs of the sinner, open to trust in forgiveness. As Girolamo Savonarola (1452–1498) affirmed in one of his homiletic commentaries, "now the fear of sin that I discover in myself makes me desperate, now the hope of your mercy sustains me. But because your mercy is greater than my misery, I will not cease to hope."

In the Bible sin is always seen as a personal act that arises from human freedom and offends the divine will. The exemplary confession that tradition puts on the lips of David after his adultery with Bathsheba and the indirect murder of her husband Uriah, Psalm 51, which has become famous as the Miserere: "Against thee, thee only, have I sinned, and done that which is evil in thy sight" (v. 4, RSV). In a dissolve we see the hand of Adam who, in the responsibility of his freedom, is raising himself up to take the fruit of the tree of the knowledge of good and evil, deciding the moral norm by himself instead of receiving it from God. Moreover, in the incipit of the *Miserere* (vv. 1–3), we dive into the entire Hebrew lexicon of sin, which describes it as "rebellion," "revolt" (*pesha'*) against God, as "missing the target" (*hatta'ah*) and "deviation" (*'awôn*). Sin is, therefore, an aberration that distances us from God. It is the rupturing of a relationship, it is a wandering from the right path in the journey of existence, it is a luminous destination that draws us far away. As an important commentator on the Psalter, Franz Delitzsch (1813–1890) wrote, sin is "the inversion of that which is good, the distortion and fracturing of that which is upright, the caricature of that which is beautiful."

Precisely in the wake of this spatial symbolism of the twisting of the destination and loss of the center, conversion is, in the Bible, a "return" (*shûb*) to the lost path, a correction of course, a free and personal decision that erases the negative decision of "distancing" from God, and, in the biblical language of the New Testament, an inversion of mentality (*metánoia*). Exemplary is the fabric of words that supports the splendid parable of the rebellious son and the loving father narrated by Luke in chapter 15: the young man "went outside of his country" (*apedémesen*) into a remote region (15:13); he then "returned" to himself in conversion (15:17): "I will arise and go to my father ... And he arose and came to his father" (15:18, 20, RSV), who twice evokes the adventure of sin and conversion in these words: "my son was dead, and has returned to life; he was lost, and is found" (15:24, 32).

Saint Paul would have recourse to another form of symbolism in the spirit of the nuptial metaphor used by the prophets for the covenant between God and his people: "God has reconciled us to himself through Christ and has entrusted to us the ministry of reconciliation. It was God who, in fact, in Christ was reconciling the world to himself, not imputing the guilt of their trespasses to men, and entrusting to us the message of reconciliation. So we are ambassadors in the name of Christ, God himself making his appeal through us. We beseech you on behalf of Christ, be reconciled to God" (2 Cor 5:18–20). Paul therefore takes up the mission entrusted to Peter and the apostles of "binding and loosing" (Mt 16:19; 18:18) and of "absolving/forgiving sins" (Jn 20:23) and reformulates it in the juridical language of "reconciliation" (*katallaghé* in Greek), the juridical act that attempts to "reconcile" (*katallássein*) the two spouses in conflict.

On this mission, which is at the basis of the sacrament of "reconciliation," must also be modeled the work of fraternal correction that all the disciples must carry out, as Saint James recalls in the "spatial" image of sin and conversion: "My brethren, if any one among you wanders from the truth and someone brings him back, let him know that whoever brings back a sinner from the error of his way will save his soul from death and will cover a multitude of sins" (James 5:19–20, RSV).

At the root of conversion, however, is always grace, expressed in forgiveness, as Pascal reminded us above. Of course, in conversion as well, the encounter between the two freedoms is necessary. Human freedom is indispensable: *j'ai pleuré et j'ai cru*, "I wept and I believed," as René de Chateaubriand (1768–1848) pithily described his conversion. Nonetheless, the love of God who forgives is fundamental: he makes it so that "though your sins are like scarlet, they shall be as white as snow; though they are red like crimson, they shall become like wool" (Is 1:18, RSV).

Well then, for this reflection on forgiveness we must entrust ourselves to another penitential Psalm, the *De Profundis*, number 130, a genuine lighted lamp that makes hope blossom again after the night of spiritual death, and, according to the Christian funereal tradition, even after the darkness of physical death. In the original Hebrew it has only fifty-two words including the particles, words of supplication that arise from the infernal whirlpools of evil and sin. These draw together around the themes of sin, forgiveness, and redemption, and the accent is entirely on the luminous horizon of forgiveness, a genuine resurrection "out of the depths."

Three subjects for meditation emerge spontaneously from the text of the Psalm. Of course, the sense of sin is always strong: "If thou, O Lord, shouldst mark iniquities, Lord, who could stand?" (v.3, RSV). But the primacy belongs to forgiveness, and here we find the first interesting annotation: "But there is forgiveness with thee, that thou mayest be feared" (v. 4). Fear is generated in the sinner not by condemnation, but by forgiveness. Why should this annotation be surprising? The answer is implicit and profound: more than the anger of God, what must provoke fear and sorrow is his infinite and disarming love that we have wounded. It is more cruel and terrible to strike a tender father than an implacable sovereign. Here as well there returns to shine the star of *charis/caritas*, the loving divine grace that sparkles in forgiveness. This is why Bernanos was correct when he wrote: "Hell is cold, even if one speaks of infernal fire, because hell means not loving anymore."

A second motif of reflection is offered to us by the image of the sentinels that describes the tension of sin in anticipation of forgiveness: "I hope for the Lord, my soul hopes, and I await his word; my soul waits for the Lord more than watchmen for the dawn, more than watchmen for the dawn" (vv. 5–6). The repetition of the image is intended to create the atmosphere of tension that is experienced on the nighttime rounds through the deserted streets of the city. There are, however, some who think that the Hebrew *shomrîm*, literally "watchmen," refers to the priests "keeping watch" in the temple (cf. Ps 134:1), in anticipation of the dawn and the celebration of the rituals and sacrifices. If we think, then, of the elevated number of priests and the system of drawing lots that was intended to permit all the members of the priestly class to preside by turns over the worship, which happened rarely (cf. Lk 1:5, 8–9), we will be able to give the tension a further, mystical connotation.

If we want to bring the image up to date, we will have to compare the state of mind of the one who hopes in divine forgiveness to that of the Catholic priest on the night before his priestly ordination. A profound shudder must therefore pervade the heart of the sinner anticipating the smiling face of the Father who forgives. We could place on his lips the opening of the penitential supplication for the synagogue on Yom Kippur, the initial words of which are: "You stretch out your hand to sinners and your arms are open to welcome the repentant . . . and to accept our sincere repentance like a sacrifice of sweet perfume . . ."

A third and final consideration is merited by the end of the Psalm, which extends to the whole community: "O Israel, hope in the Lord! For with the Lord there is love, and with him is redemption. And he will redeem Israel from all his iniquities" (vv. 7–8). Before it was the "I" of the worshiper, now it is the "we" of the whole community. Personal salvation is situated within "ecclesial" salvation. All forgiveness is inserted within the big picture of the covenant of God with the people "redeemed" from slavery in Egypt. Having escaped from the infernal abyss, the worshiper now finds himself in the assembly of the temple where the two luminous divine virtues are presented, nearly personified: *hesed*, or loving and merciful fidelity, and *pedût*, redemption, the ransom that the father pays for his child who has fallen into misery. The worshiper has recognized his fault that has drawn him toward the abyss of evil and death; but he knows that the divine grandeur does not consist of a cold, majestic, and imperial sanctity, but rather in a warm and sweet goodness that enfolds the repentant sinner.

One day a man asked a Muslim mystic of the eighth century, Rabi'a, to whom we have already referred: "I have committed many sins: if I repent, will God forgive me?" Rabi'a replied: "No, you will repent if God forgives you." This is a powerful reference to the primacy of divine grace that makes sacramental confession much different from a session of psychotherapy. This is what our Psalm also extols, and is also proclaimed by St. Paul: "Wretched man that I am! Who will deliver me from this body of death? Thanks be to God through Jesus Christ our Lord!" (Rom 7:24–25, RSV).

This, however, does not exclude the choice of human freedom to "wait for" forgiveness, to desire it, long for it, hope for it, and frankly precisely as in the prayer of one Russian spiritual master, the fifteenth century, Orthodox saint Nilus of Sora, in his Penitential Oration: "I stand before you, confused in my conscience and in silence, because my words pollute the air. Lord, grant me the tears that I do not have now to wash my sins and give me the freedom to speak to you. On the day of your last and just judgment, do not reveal my evil works before angels and men, but tear out the pages that enumerate my sins and let no one know them! So be it, Lord!"

CHAPTER XII

ABSENCE AND NOTHINGNESS

Man without God

Abbé Cénabre is a priest who has fallen into the abyss of unbelief. His story, narrated by Bernanos in the novel *L'imposture* (1927), is summarized by the writer in two words that we often consider synonymous, "absence" and "nothingness." Bernanos wrote: "Temptation is training for us, doubt is a torment. He [the abbé Cénabre], however, was not tormented by temptation. Between his trials and his cry of 'I do not believe any more!' was the difference that distinguishes absence from nothingness. Its place is not empty; there is nothing there." In fact, the empty place at table in our home is in reality the sign that someone is missing—father, mother, or spouse—who is mourned, who is remembered, who is awaited. And so it is for God. In the minds and hearts of many there is no longer an absence that can generate nostalgia, there is no space that is empty but open to question, and therefore to awaiting God, there is simply nothingness.

Another French writer, Pierre Reverdy (1889–1960), came to the point of saying that in reality "there are sometimes atheists of a ferocious bitterness who, all in all, are more interested in God than certain frivolous and casual believers are." Thus an author like the French-Romanian Emil Cioran (1911–1995) confessed that he "spied" on God's movements, finding him concealed in the music of Bach, although continuing to declare himself inscribed among the "race of the atheists." Another non-believing writer, the Russian Aleksandr Zinovyev (1922–2006), however, prayed like this: "I beseech you, my God, try to exist, at least a little for me, open your eyes, I beseech you! Oh Lord, try to follow what is happening, make an effort to see, I pray you! To live without witnesses, what a hell! Because of this, straining my voice, I cry out, I howl: My Father, I beseech you and I pray: exist!" The same thing had been said by the poet Giorgio Caproni (1912–1990): "Ah, my God, My God, / why do you not exist? / Almighty God, try (strain) by means of insisting—at least to exist."

The danger of indifference, which is the mark of contemporary society, is instead that of ignoring, of remaining inert and simply repeating the assertion in the Psalms of those without God, repeated twice in the Psalter, in numbers 14 and 53: "There is no God!" This is certainly not a matter of the vehement *Requiem aeternam Deo* intoned by Nietzsche in *The Gay Science* (1887): "God is dead! God is dead! We have killed him!" in a cry that would afterward explode into a drama.

The affirmation of the *nabal*, the "fool" of Psalm 14, is instead a sort of anticipation of contemporary indifference, of that nothingness which is not so much theoretical and metaphysical as practical and ethical. In fact, for the *nabal* God is not here, in our history, relegated as he is to a golden heaven, closed off in his eternal apathy. This is why one can abandon oneself with impunity to immorality, to "abominable deeds . . . to eat bread devouring my people" (vv. 1, 4). This paints a picture of a choice of life that disregards any transcendental presence and value, according to which they "call evil good and good evil, who put darkness for light and light for darkness, who put bitter for sweet and sweet for bitter," as Isaiah says (5:20, RSV). It is not the Truth in itself, which precedes and surpasses us, that acts as the guiding star of conduct, but the individual who weaves, like a spider, from his depths the web of various and variable certainties. The truth is no longer that sea in which one immerses oneself in order to discover ever new horizons, it is no longer that plain over which one runs in search of the chariot of the soul, to use the famous myth of the *Phaedrus* by Plato. It is, instead, a Medusa of a thousand faces that, according to circumstances and interests, changes and adapts itself.

The practical "atheism" denounced by the Psalmist, a negation of the very salvation history that includes a God who is involved and present in human affairs, is therefore the attestation of a void that is nothingness. Different, however, is the absence of God, which even the believer experiences with turmoil and distress. The supreme model is precisely in the father of biblical faith, Abraham, with his agonizing ascent of the rocky and thorny slope of Mount Moriah (Gen 22), a text that the philosopher Kierkegaard wonderfully recreated and commented on in his *Fear and Trembling* (1843). Faith also includes absence, silence, dismay: is it not true that God himself gave to Abraham his son Isaac? And now why does he demand his death? Abraham must be ready to renounce his carnal son Isaac, considered as a sort of concrete test of the divine promise, which made faith a purely rational and experiential reality.

For this reason, God asks him to cut that tie: Abraham is now ready to renounce the immediate and concrete Isaac-test, giving witness to his absolute faith, and thus descends the mountain having beside him the Isaac-divine promise.

We are, therefore, in front of the essential paradigm of faith, which at its ultimate apogee is bare, having no support other than the transcendent word, the divine promise. The preceding rational steps are not denied, but it is recalled—as the Danish philosopher writes at the end of his work—that "faith is the highest passion of every man. There are perhaps in every generation many men who do not get that far, but no one goes farther." It is along these lines that we encounter a similar experience within the Psalter as well. We are in the face of a mystic in the "dark night," a prayer of the silence of God. Let us listen to some of its voices.

"To thee, O Lord, I cry out; my rock, be not deaf to me, lest, if thou be indifferent to me, I become like those who go down to the Pit" (Ps 28:1). "O God, come out of your silence; do not be silent or immobile, O God!" (Ps

83:1). Finally the temptation against faith makes inroads: "And I thought, 'It is my grief: the right hand of the Most High is paralyzed'" (Ps 77:10). The liberating hand of the Lord in the exodus is now blocked and inert like that of an elderly man. Sometimes it is the whole community that cries out to the Lord to break his lethargy: "Rouse thyself! Why sleepest thou, O Lord? . . . Why dost thou hide thy face? Why dost thou forget our affliction and oppression?" (Ps 44:23–24). "Stir up thy might, and come to save us" (Ps 80:2). "How long, O Lord? Wilt thou hide thyself for ever?" (Ps 89:46). "Be not silent, O God of my praise!" (Ps 109:1, RSV). But what has come to be seen as the ultimate song of the silence of God is Psalm 22, precisely because it came to the lips of Christ on the cross: "My God, my God, why hast thou forsaken me?" preserved by the evangelists in the Aramaic pronounced by Jesus, thus making it an *ipsissimum verbum* of his, a living reliquary of these extreme and supreme moments.

The first movement of Psalm 22's powerful supplication (vv. 1–21) has a tragic tonality, and the famous initial verses bring to the stage an absent God, like an impassible sovereign, seated on his royal throne, indifferent to our tears and to the turmoil of our history. At one time, yes, he saved our fathers, but now he is detached and silent toward us: "O my God, I cry out by day, but thou dost not answer; and by night, but I have no silence. Yet thou art holy, seated on the throne amidst the praises of Israel. In thee our fathers trusted; they trusted, and thou didst deliver them. To thee they cried, and were saved; in thee they trusted, and were not disappointed" (vv. 2–5). And immediately after this evocation of a serene past, marked by the divine presence, the worshiper contrasts a powerful "But I am a worm, and not anymore a man" (v. 6). He tries to provoke this mute God by setting an ancient and radical connection before him: "Yet thou art he who took me from the womb; thou didst keep me safe upon my mother's breasts. Upon thee was I cast from my birth, and since my mother bore me thou hast been my God" (vv. 9–10, RSV).

But then comes the horrible present described in baroque images, with impressionistic and overloaded tints, with the eruption of a pack of beasts, bulls, lions, dogs, oxen, which are replaced with a hunting scene typical of Psalmic lamentations, in which the worshiper, pursued by dogs and huntsmen, is like a wounded animal of prey, panting and almost overtaken. At this point the believer is at the point of death. At the edge of the grave he is stripped of his clothing that is divided and distributed, and he launches a last cry to the taciturn heavens: "But thou, O Lord, be not far off! O thou my strength, hasten to my aid!" (v. 19). In outline we intuit the Gospel fabric of the Passion of Christ of which this Psalm becomes a sort of prefiguration.

It is significant to set this supplication and the experience of the suffering Christ beside a realization that paradoxically is offered to us by a famous director who was an atheist but was constantly tormented by theological themes, the Swedish Ingmar Bergman. It is a way to remind us that the time of trial and absence is not empty and null, but is also fruitful, faith being not a cold and compulsory adherence to an evident theorem, but a living and transcendent person.

In the film *Winter Light* (1963), the main character is a Lutheran pastor who, losing his wife in a dramatic way, slides into unbelief, tangled in the nets of the scandal of an indifferent and mute God. It is a simple person, the sacristan, who reminds the pastor of the solidarity of Christ with regard to all of humanity that lives in the silence of God. "Think of Gethsemane, Pastor, think of the crucifixion. There all of the disciples had fallen asleep, they had understood nothing, and he remained alone even on the cross. The suffering must have been very great: to understand that no one had understood anything. But this was not the worst, Pastor. When Christ was nailed to the cross and remained there, tormented by suffering, he exclaimed: 'My God, my God, why have you abandoned me?' Christ was seized by a great doubt in the moment that preceded his death. That must have been the cruelest of the sufferings, I mean the silence of God." The pastor returns to preach in his church, now empty after his crisis of faith, and this is perhaps a sign of his rebirth.

The worshiper in Psalm 22 likewise does not allow his cry to be extinguished in nothingness. In fact, at the end of his heartrending lamentation he has a surprise: "You have answered me" (v. 24). And from that moment the elegy turns into a dance, the plea into thanksgiving to the point of exploding, in an enthusiastic crescendo, into a festive hymn for the Lord, who is indeed king but is not indifferent to the suffering of his creature (vv. 28–31). So a song that began with the Passion ends with Easter.

A lay theologian, Sergio Quinzo, wrote: "Just as there can be no consolation without sorrow, so there can be no perfect sorrow that is not consoled." According to the Jewish tradition, in citing the beginning of a Psalm the intention is to evoke the text in its entirety, and therefore also the positive ending. This is why Luke hears from the lips of the dying Christ a verse of another Psalm, 31:6, a trusting interjection: "Then Jesus, crying with a loud voice, said, 'Father, into thy hands I commit my spirit!' And having said this he breathed his last" (Lk 23:46, RSV).

It is with this trust that we must wait for heaven to open for us as well on the days of our Mount Moriah, in the silent and empty hours, in the certainty that our pleas will not fall into nothingness and in the end will receive a mysterious reply. This reply is not only the echo of our cry, but the subtle voice of the Father who does not give his child serpents and scorpions (Lk 11:12).

We began this chapter with the testimony of one "without God," Abbé Cénabre. Let us conclude with another "atheist" who instead was tormented by the absence of God. It is the famous playwright Eugène Ionesco. In an interview, asked about his religious quest, he resorted to paradox: "I rush to the phone every time it rings, in the hope, disappointed every time, that it could be God who is calling me. Or at least one of his angel secretaries." But on the last page of his diary, the day before his death, March 27, 1994, he wrote this line: "Pray. I do not know to whom. I hope to Jesus Christ."

CHAPTER XIII

WISDOM IS SAVOR

The Wise and Happy Man

Having been made a member of the Institut de France, the philosopher and critic Roland Barthes (1915–1980) gave his inaugural *lectio* on a category that he himself considered outdated, "wisdom," and he defined it like this: "Wisdom is no power, a little knowledge, a little intelligence, and as much flavor as possible." The word in fact comes from the Latin verb *sápere*, the primary meaning of which is to "have flavor." In this light he continued with humility: "There is an age at which one teaches what one knows; but then comes another at which one teaches what one does not know: this is called seeking." In the previous reflection we encountered the arrogant voice of the *nabal*, the "fool," who, denying God, feels entitled to rage against his neighbor, there being no transcendent moral law. Now, instead, let us bring to the stage his antithesis: the wise man, the biblical *hakam*, whose prayers permeate the Psalter.

It is precisely the gate of entrance to the collection of the Psalms, Psalm 1, that presents for meditation the antithetical couple of misbeliever and believer, impious and just, fool and wise man. Two portraits that embody a classical module in many cultures, that of the "two ways": "But the path of the righteous is like the light of dawn, which shines brighter and brighter until full day. The way of the wicked is like deep darkness" (Prov 4:18–19, RSV). Each of us is brought to the crossroads from which these two ways diverge: "I have set before you this day life and good on the one side, death and evil on the other blessing and curse; therefore choose..." (Dt 30:15, 19). This choice is described in the opening of our Psalm. What appears first is the horizon of perversion. The Psalmist deftly portrays the psychology of temptation and fall through a verbal trilogy: "Blessed is the man who does not enter into union with the wicked, nor stands in the way of sinners, nor sits in the assembly of scoffers" (Ps 1:1).

The first act is a simple "entrance," a "following" according to a superficial curiosity in the attraction that evil exercises on everyone. Then the second moment: this is the more lasting "lingering," stopping to listen. From here one falls into lasting acquiescence, habitual coexistence: by now the man is "seated" in an intentional fellowship in the assembly of the wicked. But then there appears the other path, antithetical to the path of the misbeliever who does not recognize any divine law. For the wise man, in fact, "he finds his delight in the law of the Lord, and on his law he meditates day and night" (v. 2). It is therefore the Torah, the Word of God that "[makes] wise the mind" (Ps 19:7). The Psalmist implicitly plants a question in the mind of the person who reads his song: Which side are you on? Has the fascination of evil subtly ensnared you? Or does your heart beat for truth and justice, and is your face illuminated by the divine light?

To further encourage the choice of wisdom, goodness, and the Word of God, he depicts another duality, this time taken from the world of plant life and cultivation. On one side is a picture of great freshness, previously "painted" by Jeremiah as well (17:7–8): the wise man will be "like a tree planted by a stream of water, that yields its fruit in its season, and its leaf never wither" (Ps 1:3). In a sun-drenched desert stands a luxuriant tree full of fruit: beside it flows a stream whose waters moisten its roots. On the other side is the opposite picture set on a farm at harvest time. The paddle tosses the grain into the air so that the chaff can be blown away: the wicked "are like chaff which the wind drives away" (v. 4, RSV). One is reminded of the words of the Baptist about Christ: "His winnowing fork is in his hand, to clear his threshing floor, and to gather the wheat into his granary, but the chaff he will burn with unquenchable fire" (Lk 3:17, RSV).

The solidity and fruitfulness of the tree is contrasted with the vacuity and aridity of the chaff, volatile and unsubstantial. The figure of the just man in the Christian tradition will be turned into the Just and Wise One without equal, Christ, and the symbolic tree—as Saint Justin teaches—will become the tree of the cross, "the wood that bears fruit for us with the waters of baptism." Our life remains, however, clearly under scrutiny: we often perform vain and vacuous works, searching for personal prestige or generated by unconfessable motives of pride, prevarication, and anxiety for success. It is not necessarily evil, but a superficiality and lack of substance, the multiplication of external actions and things. People were surprised that Socrates visited the marketplace of Athens so often. To those who asked him why he did so, he replied: "I go to see all of the things that I do not need!" This chaff of vanity and banality, foolishness and ignorance is contrasted with the vigor and seriousness of the tree of wisdom. The Austrian writer Robert Musil (1880–1942), in his masterpiece *The Man Without Qualities*, wrote: "There does not exist even one idea that stupidity has not been able to put to use; it is quick and versatile and can put on all the garments of the truth. The truth, however, has only one garment and one path, and it is always at a disadvantage."

At this point we would like to propose a second reflection that we link closely to the symbolic, and therefore global, conception that biblical wisdom has of reality. As one reads in the first "priestly" account of creation, every creature is *tôb*, meaning "good/beautiful." Ethics and aesthetics are interwoven, goodness and beauty are sisters. It comes spontaneously, then, to understand why the Psalter invites us to "sing praises with a psalm" (Ps 47:7, RSV), and in Hebrew we have an exquisitely sapiential term, *maskîl*, that among other things recurs in thirteen titles of Psalms and that the Vulgate renders as *psallite sapienter*. So it is necessary to pray in a manner that is wise in content and beautiful in form. In the letter,

addressed to the clergy, that accompanied his *Disserta-
tio de Psalmis*, the famous bishop of Meaux, Jacques-Bé-
nigne Bossuet (1627–1704), admonished that "to sing
wisely to God one must learn ever more with erudition
and intelligence."

In this way, a very complex and delicate thematic
chapter is opened before us, that of sacred music, which
the titles added to the Psalms evoke with the indication
of mood, instrumentation, and technical musical terms
for performance. Let us allow to resound within us, then,
Psalm 150, the final doxology of the Psalter, the singing
of the final alleluia, sectioned in cascades like the alleluias
of Händel's *Messiah*. The common thread of the prayers
of the 150 Psalms, imbued with many lamentations and
few joys, pervaded by the breath of life, the bustle of the
world, and even by the cries of battle, is joined to the liturgy and becomes the free and serene praise of God. To
this celebration in the temple is also called the orchestra
made up of seven instruments: the trumpet, the harp, the
lute, the timbrel, various stringed instruments, the flute,
and the cymbals.

To these are added both ritual dancing (Ps 118:27
also called to "bind the festal procession with branches")
and a living instrument: the breath of every living being,
which is not only the sound of the woodwinds of the
orchestra, nor only the voice of the choir, but also the
breath of every creature, as the Jewish book of the Hag-
gadah suggested in an exemplary homiletic story. In it
David is proud of his lyre, the texts of his psalms, and
his singing, and a frog responds to him with its croaking:

"David, do not be puffed up! I sing more than you do, with my whole self, in honor of God!" Also within Judaism, Elie Wiesel, who received the Nobel peace prize in 1986, affirmed that the angels, after having appeared to Jacob ascending and descending upon a ladder that united heaven and earth (Gn 28:10–22), forgot to pull it up again. This is the musical scale that can lead us from earth to heaven.

The Psalms are poetry, song, and music, and therefore they follow the *via pulchritudinis* to pray to and speak of God, "splendid and magnificent" (cf. Ps 76:5). In the first book of Chronicles the singers and musicians also received—like Bezalel, the craftsman of the ark of the covenant and of the holy tent with its furniture (Ex 31:3–5)—an "inspiration" of the Spirit of God, so much so that the Hebrew term which indicates a musical performance also indicates prophetic activity, *nb'* (1 Cr 25:1). Beauty and faith are sisters because both of them are seeking the infinite and the eternal, since art—as the painter Paul Klee observes—does not represent the visible, but the Invisible that is in the visible. And as then-cardinal Ratzinger wrote in 2002, "beauty pulls us up short, but in so doing it reminds us of our final destiny." Now, resorting to an etymological assonance, we could say that the wound inflicted by art upon humanity is a "window" open to the absolute, the transcendent, the divine. The French poet Paul Valéry (1871–1945) recalled that "the painter must not depict what he sees, but what he will see." Like faith, art must lead us to eschatology, which is the fullness of meaning.

But art is also a wound in the living body. It creates tension, even suffering, like when a scab is opened in our flesh. Another great painter like Georges Braque (1882–1963) recognized that "art is made to disturb, while science reassures us." One cannot come away unscathed from the contemplation of a painting by Caravaggio or Michelangelo's Judgment in the Sistine Chapel. The dismay of the crucified Peter or the descent from on high of the divine arm and hand that wants to "catch," "grasp" (cf. Ph 3:12) the blinded Paul on the road to Damascus that Michelangelo painted in the Pauline Chapel are a provocative depiction of the divine vocation that turns life upside-down. The disquiet that a wound generates in the body is a symbol of the disquiet of art and faith in the sense of the celebrated motto of Augustine: *Inquietum est cor nostrum donec requiescat in te.* The common destination of beauty and faith is, in fact, the divine infinite that for art is a vortex of light and for faith is a person who is waiting for you. And to reach this destination, which is beyond the senses and beyond rationality itself, "inspiration" or grace is needed.

The liturgy must return—albeit in the new grammar that contemporary art, music, and architecture have adopted (one need think only of what happened when the monodic purity of Gregorian chant was replaced with the interweaving of polyphonic voices)—to being the seat of beauty that begins with faith, reverberating at the same time the presence of God, the supreme beauty. One should be able to repeat the suggestion of Saint John Damascene, who invited the pagan wanting to learn about the Christian faith to enter a church and contemplate the icons, the images, and the sacred scenes.

The liturgy, a bit like art, is mystery and unveiling, it is transcendence and illumination. Genuine liturgical action is not only "mysterical" with the risk of esoteric sacralism, but neither is it only congregational intelligibility, with the risk of trivialization into a social gathering. With the words of Benedict XVI in front of the artists who had come from all over the world in 2009 to the Sistine Chapel, let us conclude by recalling that art and faith reveal the meaning of history and of life: art "is movement and ascent, a continuing tension towards fullness, towards human happiness, towards a horizon that always transcends the present moment even as the two coincide."

CHAPTER XIV

THE SONG OF THE PRIESTS

The Immortal Man

"O house of Aaron, put your trust in the Lord! He is their help and their shield . . . The Lord is mindful of us; he will bless us; he will bless the house of Israel; he will bless the house of Aaron . . . Let the house of Aaron say, 'His steadfast love endures for ever' . . . O house of Israel, bless the Lord! O house of Aaron, bless the Lord!" (Ps 115:10, 12; 118:3; 135:19). These are some Psalmic fragments that emerge from the setting of the temple of Zion, in which are situated the entire Psalter, the presence and voice of the priests. For these priests we reserve now the role of protagonist, entrusting to them two songs in which their voice seems to resound, even with an autobiographical touch. We have already met one of them who, in Psalm 42–43, narrated his sorrowful experience of expulsion from the temple, isolated and embittered in a land of exile, but with his heart burning with the desire to be readmitted into the priestly assembly of Zion.

So we will collect two new testimonies, but with a single message, a "Paschal" message of immortality in communion with God, already foretasted in the present liturgy. The first to come forward for us is the author of Psalm 16, who immediately proclaims a profession of love for the Lord: "I said Lord, 'Thou art my Lord; thou art my good, above thee, I have no one'" (v. 2). He also pronounces, however, a confession of fault for a sinful past, marked by the fascination of idolatry: "To the sacred idols of the country, to the powerful gods went all of my favor . . . But I will no longer pour out their libations of blood, on my lips I will no longer put their names" (vv. 3–4). Indeed, even the priest is a fragile person with his baggage of faults and miseries that are waiting for divine forgiveness and conversion. At this point the psalmist priest presents the heart of his ministry, the total decision for God, belonging to him and in his service.

Let us listen to the literal version of this symbolic autobiographical profile of the priest: "The Lord is the portion and my cup attributed to me, you preserve my lot. The cords of measurement have fallen for me in a delicious place, yes, splendid is my inheritance" (vv. 5–6). In the Bible this pictorial lexicon is typical of the priestly class which, in the tribal partition of the Promised Land, did not obtain any territory of its own. Those who were consecrated to worship had to avoid interfering in politics and the management of the structure of society, but had to be the intermediary with God in the life of the people, in freedom from any concrete tie or interest, living only on the tithes offered by the community for the support of the ministers of God. The various symbols used by the priest, connected to the language of the division of the land of Canaan, express precisely this totality of dedication to mission. This obtains from God a generous recompense, even in concrete terms.

The Lord is, in fact, "the portion attributed," the true inheritance of the priest and not a plot of land, as had happened for the other tribes. The Lord is his "cup," meaning the one who hosts and welcomes him as a relative by assigning him a serene destiny, symbolized precisely by the cup of hospitality. The Lord is the "lot" of the priest: not a possession received in a drawing, as happened for the territories of the tribes, but a destiny of fullness and beauty given by God. The Lord is "his delicious place," obtained through "the cords of measurement" of the tribal terrains: one intuits in this image the temple, the seat of the human and religious life of the priest. Finally, the Lord is the "splendid inheritance," the supreme good to be protected. Saint Augustine commented in *Sermone* 334: "The Psalmist does not say: 'O God, give me an inheritance!' He says instead: 'All that you can give me apart from you is vile. Be yourself my inheritance. You are the one that I love . . .' To hope for God from God, to be filled with God from God. He is enough for you, outside of him nothing can be enough for you."

At this point, in front of the psalmist priest, the curtain opens on the future beyond death. In his famous novel *Il fu Mattia Pascal* (1904), Luigi Pirandello wrote: "We cannot understand life, if in some way we do not explain death to ourselves. The directive criterion of our actions, the thread for emerging for this labyrinth, the light must come to us from there, from death." For our priest this is true, but so is the contrary: the present illuminates our ultimate destiny. If we are already in communion with God who is the Eternal, we are already foretasting the otherworldly life. Saint John affirmed this when he reported the words of Jesus in the nighttime encounter with Nicodemus: "For God so loved the world that he gave his only Son, that whoever believes in him should not perish but have eternal life" (Jn 3:16, RSV). God's embrace of love pulls us from mortality and introduces us to blessed immortality. Dostoevsky wrote in *Demons* (1871): "If I have begun to love God and have rejoiced in his love, is it possible that he would extinguish me and my joy and reduce me to zero? If there is God who loves me, I too am immortal!"

In the Muslim mystical tradition, when the angel of death presents himself to Abraham, the patriarch reacts by asking: "Can a friend perhaps desire the death of a friend?" The Arabic title of Abraham is el-Khalil, the friend of God. But then comes the reply of the angel: "Does a friend not perhaps desire the full encounter with his friend?" And this is why the cemetery, in the same Muslim tradition, is called "the house of the Encounter."

Let us listen to the voice of our priest who sings of the ultimate harbor of that intimacy already tasted in the temple, when he will come to the threshold of death: "You will not abandon my life to Sheol (the netherworld), nor will you let your faithful see the Pit. You will show me the path of life; fullness of joy in your presence, in your right hand are pleasures for evermore" (vv. 10–11). It almost seems that one can hear in the background the promise of Christ: "I am going to prepare a place for you, I will come again and will take you with me, that where I am you may be also" (Jn 14:3).

Now the second priest takes the stage, the author of Psalm 73, that marvelous "story of a soul" or "song of the heart" (because of the recurrence of this word in the text). He too recounts his autobiographical experience, which includes a period of crisis. The source of this temptation to abandon the faith is the scandal of triumphant injustice without the intervention of God. This gives a profile of the powerful wicked man of great emotional impact: his life is continual enjoyment, his pride adorns him like a necklace, his garment is violence, his mouth defies heaven and earth, his heart is a den of follies, his fatness generates nausea, his followers drink in subserviently all of his foolishness and blasphemy (vv. 4–9). The feet of the just man "trip" over the stumbling block of arrogant and victorious immorality. He confesses, in fact: "All in vain have I kept my heart clean and washed my hands in innocence" (v. 13, RSV), but then "all the day long I have been stricken, and chastened every morning" (v. 14, RSV). Strong is the temptation of conforming to the way of life of the wicked: "I will speak like them" (v. 15, RSV).

But then comes the breakthrough. The priest enters into the "sanctuary of God" (v. 17, RSV): the Hebrew locution used (*miqdeshê-'el*) is however more fluid, it can also indicate a mystical experience of meditation on the divine "mysteries" or the Word of the Lord. It is certain that in that atmosphere of faith and under that light "I understood what will be their 'aharît," the ultimate destiny of the perverse: they will slide into the infernal pit, their destination is perdition, their splendor only an illusion. For the faithful there opens, instead, a glorious horizon. Free from the temptation of success, of wealth, and of power that had drawn him like a beast (v. 22), he renews his profession of faith and love, happy to have the Lord for his hereditary "portion," precisely as proclaimed by the priest of Psalm 16. The freedom, gratuitousness, purity, and spirituality of authentic belief in God are the only true recompense awaited: "Having you, there is nothing upon earth that I desire" (v. 25).

His witness is limpid and absolute: "For me it is good to be near God" (v. 28). The Hebrew, however, is much more intense, because *tôb* also suggests beauty, happiness, pleasure, while "being near" indicates profound adherence, embracing and being united in a total intimacy. This communion generates the certainty of immortality, which is described in the same tonality as Psalm 16: "Nevertheless I am continually with thee; thou dost hold my right hand, thou wilt guide me with thy counsel, and afterward thou wilt receive me to glory . . . even if my flesh and my heart fail, the rock of my heart and my portion is God for ever" (vv. 23–24, 26).

It is significant that it should be two priests who split open the eschatological horizon. In fact, among the worshipers of the Psalter there are many brothers of ours who are waiting for a "beyond," which they do not glimpse except in the shadow of Sheol, where existence becomes spectral and without light and life. Precisely because of these hesitant biblical presences, we must welcome and support with respect our uncertain and doubting brothers and those who, in desperation of their existence, are like the singer of Psalm 88, called by some exegetes "pessimism's Song of Solomon," the only Psalmic supplication that does not end with a ray of hope. In fact, the constant thread of suffering, solitude, nightmares, hostility, silence of God and of friends that permeates his life results only in death and the last phrase whispered in this extreme plea launched to God is: "My companions are only darkness" (88:19).

Besides this sigh of death there is, however, loud and clear the truly "paschal" message of the priests: the New Testament sees in Psalm 16 a proclamation of the resurrection of Christ (Acts 2:22–28; 13:35–37). This proclamation must be sounded out loud in a society that tends to remove the question about death, entrusting itself, if anything, to the illusion of living without growing old, to the dream of technological immortality, so much so that the Canadian sociologist Céline Lafontaine spoke in one of her books, emblematically entitled *The Dream of Eternity* (2008), of a "postmortal" society, while the journalist Catherine Mayer proposed the definition of an "amortal" humanity ("Amortality" was the title of her 2009 article). The result is, instead, the solitude of the dying person: "never as today have men died so silently and hygienically, and never have they been so alone," Norbert Elias wrote in 1985, delineating a death without hope similar to the one described in the unforgettable *The Death of Ivan Ilyich* by Tolstoy.

The ancient worshiper in Psalm 49 had already swept away the illusions of technology and economic power, admonishing that "however high maybe the ransom you pay for life it can never suffice, that he should continue to live without end, and never see the Pit" (vv. 8–9). With realism the Psalmist repeated that "man, in spite of his riches, cannot last, he is like the beasts that perish" (v. 12). There is one path to victory over death, that which the psalmist priests presented, rooting it in their experience of faith and which the praying poet of Psalm 49 reiterates: "Yes, only God can ransom me, it will be only he who with certitude will pull me out from the power of Sheol," (v. 15). This ransoming begins now, when man unites himself with the Lord of time, with the Eternal and Immortal King of ages, living in intimacy with him. Because of this, as Blessed John Henry Newman exhorted, "fear not that thy life shall come to an end, but rather that it shall never have a beginning." In that extreme moment, which is however also a new beginning, to use a beautiful verse of the writer Cesare Pavese—whose existence however ended tragically in suicide—"death will come and it will have your eyes." For the believer, it will be the gaze of the eyes of God.

CHAPTER XV

AROUND A FESTIVE TABLE

Man, Family, the Elderly

"I think, Lord, that you have had enough of people who talk about serving you with the look of a commander, of knowing you with the air of a professor, of loving you as one loves in an old marriage. One day when you wanted something different, you invented Saint Francis, and you made him your minstrel. Allow us to invent something in order to be happy people who dance our lives with you." She confessed: "At the age of fifteen I was strictly an atheist and found the world more absurd every day." But suddenly in her life something happened that she calls "dazzling," and her existence became a total donation for her humiliated and resentful brothers of the dilapidated Parisian quarter of Ivry. We have given voice to Madeleine Delbrêl (1904–1964) to introduce the "laypeople" of the Psalter, after having heard the message of the priests.

Even shepherds have to live with their flocks in a loving and joyful way. Now, in the Psalter there is a pageant of all ages, classes, situations. There is the pregnant mother (139:13), the mother with her child (131:2), one hears the little ones and the nursing babies who already praise the divine magnificence (8:2), sons are raised fresh and robust "like plants well grown right from their youth," the slender and elegant daughters "like corner pillars chiseled to adorn a palace" (144:12). And young women and men, together with the preceding generation of parents and grandparents, intone their alleluia to God accompanied even by the political class: "Kings of the earth and all peoples, princes and all rulers of the earth! Young men and maidens together, old men and children! Let them praise the name of the Lord" (148:11–13). In a certain sense, it is our "Sunday" liturgical assembly, which sees the community gathered before God with its various personal and collective stories, brought to the Lord and transformed into sacrificial offering, into praise and supplication.

Our gaze is now fixed on two figures present in that assembly. On one side is a beautiful family with parents and children, the heritage of the Lord and his reward as Psalm 127 says, depicting the scene of a father sur-rounded by his sons like arrows of defense and support (vv. 4–5). Clement of Alexandria (2nd–3rd century) in his *Protrepticus*, examined a well-known remark of Jesus: "Who are the two or three gathered in the name of Christ, in the midst of whom stands the Lord?" And he replied: "Are they not perhaps the man, the woman, and the child, since the two spouses are united by God?" On the other side are the elderly, who often constitute the more substantial presence in the life of a Christian community. Let us begin, then, to compile the story of a happy family. This is recounted to us by Psalm 128, a sapiential "beatitude" ("Blessed is the one who fears the Lord . . .") that delineates the exemplary family model, to the point that it has become a responsorial Psalm in the Catholic marriage liturgy and in the *ketubbôt*, the Jewish parchments that seal a marriage. We all have a family behind us, and we are all aware that this—in spite of the crises, the criticisms, even the deformations, the degenerations, and the devastations that it undergoes— remains a pillar of society, as the anthropologist Claude Lévi-Strauss (1908–2009) observes: "The family as a more or less lasting union, socially approved, of a man, a woman, and their children . . . is a universal phenomenon, found in every and any type of society."

The Psalm depicts a family at home on a feast day. As the writer Jorge Luis Borges (1899–1986) said, "every home is a candelabra on which the lives burn with separate flames"; the family is, therefore, like a *flama aislada*, a flame isolated behind the walls of a house, the warmth of which must however be transmitted outside. Unfortunately, this often does not happen because the emblem of contemporary society is the locked door that excludes all contact, even with the neighbors. The fear of the other, individualism, and solitude immerse that flame in an asphyxiating atmosphere that extinguishes it, or by completely isolating it makes it explode and burn those who are around it. But a different climate reigns in the model family that the forty-five Hebrew words of Psalm 128 depict with sweetness and intensity.

First comes the father, who supports the family with his work, a dramatic theme in our time because of its precariousness or absence: "You shall eat the fruit of the labor of your hands; you shall be happy, and it shall be well with you" (v. 2, RSV). Man is supremely a laborer, placed on the earth to "cultivate and care for it," and to give names to animals and things, which means to understand and govern them, as chapter two of Genesis teaches. So the husband and father is seated at a lavish table: beside him is his wife, who is like a "fruitful vine" with whom one lives "the intimacy of the home" (v. 3, RSV). Just as a rich vine full of clusters of grapes signifies life and prosperity, so also does the fruitful and cheerful woman. With her the husband lives that "intimacy which expresses itself in always being able to combine sexuality with tenderness, *eros* with sentiment and passion, while still placing at the center the golden knot of love in mutual and total donation.

One thus has truly "one flesh" in the intimate embrace of persons, in the reciprocal transfusion of sentiments and thoughts, because—as chapter two of Genesis also says—woman is "a homologous, corresponding help," *kenegdô*, who literally "stands in front" of man in an equality of gazes, eye to eye, by which the tears of one are turned into the sorrow of the other, and the laughter of one becomes the joy of the other. The Talmud very wisely warns, and the warning is valid above all in the face of violence perpetrated against women even in our day: "Be very careful lest you make a woman weep, for God counts her tears! Woman came from the rib of man, not from the feet that she should be trodden on, nor from the head that she should be superior, but from the side so that she should be equal, a bit below the arm in order to be protected, and on the side of the heart in order to be loved."

Also seated around the table are the children, "like olive shoots" (v. 3, RSV), full of sap and vitality. An epigraph is written on the wall of this house. It defines the source of happiness, or rather of "beatitude," and is found in the opening sentence of the Psalm: "Blessed is every one who fears the Lord, who walks in his ways" (v. 1, RSV). A faith that is lived is the principle that upholds the existence of this family and makes it happy. It is the rock on which this house stands firm. This beatitude, this family joy, is sealed by the final liturgical blessing, which we could compare in sacramental terms to the sacrament of marriage: "Lo, thus shall the man be blessed who fears the Lord. The Lord bless you from Zion!" (vv. 4–5, RSV). At this point the doors of the house are opened. The believing family does not bolt the entrance and isolate itself with its joys and its problems, but goes out into the city to contribute to the good of the whole civil and ecclesial community: "May you see the prosperity of Jerusalem all the days of your life" (v. 5, RSV).

The gaze is extended toward the future, also thinking of the successive generations so that they might find a just and serene world, under the banner of *shalôm*, the peace that is fullness of life: "May you see your children's children! Peace be upon Israel" (v. 6, RSV). Thus the Franciscan "Peace and good!" is spread like a cloak over the city and over the entire nation. One of the "seven blessings for weddings" of the synagogue ritual offers us an opportunity to "bless" our families, so that they may reflect the exemplary model of the Psalm: "Blessed are you, Lord, who have granted to the groom and to the bride rejoicing, singing, joy, gladness, love, peace, brotherhood, friendship . . . May the jubilant voices of the groom and bride and the joyful choirs of those who accompany them in their happiness resound out loud. Blessed are you, Lord, who gladden the groom with his bride."

Within this family let us now introduce a figure who is becoming ever more relevant in our day: the grandparents. Let us do so by evoking the figure of the elderly man who in the Psalter, just as in the ancient patriarchal civilizations, has an important function at the community level. The Bible extols him, albeit in the awareness of his human frailty, not only physical but also mental (one should think of the two libidinous elderly men of the account of Susanna in Daniel 13). The just, like fruitful palm trees and mighty cedars of Lebanon, through their faith and liturgical prayer, "Still bring forth fruit in old age, they are ever full of sap and green, and they will proclaim how upright the Lord is" (Ps 92:14–15). Let us, however, make our own that song of the elderly man which is Psalm 71, an emotionally moving text because of the testimony of fidelity and hope that it reveals, becoming a sketch to delineate a spirituality of old age. This calls to mind the two Gospel figures of the elderly Simeon and the eighty-four-year-old Anna, who welcome the newborn Jesus with love, succeeding in understanding the mystery and mission concealed in that little one (Lk 2:22–38).

This elderly man casts a retrospective gaze over his past, moving beyond his youth to that initial instant of his existence which he delineates with features similar to those we have encountered in Psalm 139 on the genesis of the human creature: "For thou, O Lord God, my hope, my trust from my youth. Upon thee I have leaned from my mother's womb; thou art my heritage. My praise is continually of thee. I have been as a portent to many; but thou art my strong refuge. My mouth is filled with thy praise, and all day I sing thy splendor" (Ps 71:5–8). But this luminous past of faith and joy is opposed by a heavy and sorrowful present, made of hostility and incomprehension, of bodily decrepitude and unhappiness, presented with bitterness to God "Do not cast me off in the time of old age; forsake me not when my strength declines. For my enemies speak ill of me, those who watch for my life consult together, thinking, 'God has forsaken him; pursue and seize him, for there is none to deliver him'" (vv. 9–11).

There is perhaps the dissatisfaction that afflicts the elderly man and that has a page of extraordinary plasticity in the final song of Qoheleth (12:1–7), where is described the nausea of a fragile and miserable existence in which the body becomes like a castle in disrepair and there is already a glimpse of the frozen hand of death that is about to take hold of its victim. Our elderly worshiper, however, does not lose faith and trust, but continues: "O God, be not far from me; O my God, make haste to help me! May my accusers be put to shame and consumed; with scorn and disgrace may they be covered who seek my destruction. But I will hope continually, and will praise thee yet more and more" (vv. 12–14).

And from this moment forward, the whole Psalm gazes toward a joyous future: he will return to the temple to intone his praises to the Lord, he will again pick up the harp and the lyre and will continue to accompany his thanksgiving with music (v. 22). Then he will be able to proclaim his testimony of fidelity to God before the whole community: "Now that I am old and have gray hair, O God, do not forsake me, till I proclaim thy might to all the generations to come" (v. 18). Moreover, there is even the certainty that God will invigorate him by driving away the specter of death: "Though thou who hast made me see many sore troubles thou wilt revive me again; from the depths of the earth thou wilt bring me up again. Thou wilt increase my honor, and surround me with comfort" (vv. 20–21).

This song of the elderly man, marked by a very clear realism, maintains a freshness which makes it understandable how old age is not to be judged only as a chronological state. It is above all an existential condition: if it is supported by ideals, spiritual values, and hope, everything is transformed and even the dark tunnel of physical trials and frailty is overcome by glimpsing the final light of the Lord who does not abandon us. As the book of Wisdom says, "For venerated old age is not length of time, nor measured by number of years; but understanding is gray hair for men, and a blameless life is ripe old age" (Wis 4:8–9). It is wonderful that love for music accompanies the old age of this worshiper, and his lips still murmur songs of joy: as an ancient Tibetan hymn says, the body of the elderly man is "a precious chest of songs of faith."

CHAPTER XVI

LIKE BALM AND DEW

Man is Love

Jesus returns to the earth and, in our media-saturated time, is constantly assailed by a crowd of journalists and television operators who want above all to record his miracles. But one day "a man led to Jesus his sick daughter and said to him: 'I do not want you to heal her, I want you to love her.' So Jesus kissed the girl and said: 'In truth this man has asked for what I can give.'" This scenario was imagined by a strongly "secular" writer, Ennio Flaiano (1910–1972), who transfused into this representation his experience as a father with a daughter afflicted with epileptic encephalitis whom he loved intensely and in secret, and who survived him by twenty years. What God wants to give first of all is his love, and the Psalmist offers a stupendous divine portrait in this regard: "Thou hast kept count of my tossings; put thou my tears in thy water bag! Are they not written in thy book?" (Ps 56:8).

On the one hand, in the monumental ledger of history, the genuine registry of humanity, the Lord marks down all the steps of the life's journey of every creature, including the deviations of sin, but also notes the sufferings of the miserable and the oppressed. On the other hand, there is a nomadic image: just as the shepherd carries in his flask—his "portable well," according to the definition of the Bedouins—the water for his pasturings, so also God collects with tenderness all the tears of the suffering and keeps them in his chest, as if they were precious stones. The worshiper, who often weeps in secret, knows that his tears do not fall to the ground, soaking into the dust of the desert, but are gathered by his God. The believer must also be exemplary under this loving profile of the Lord.

In our portrait gallery of the worshiper according to the Psalter, the moment has come to draw the concluding face, the one marked by fraternal love, in the path of the appeal reiterated by Saint John: "Beloved, if God so loved us, we also ought to love one another" (1 Jn 4:11, RSV).

We will entrust ourselves to an exquisite miniature, that of Psalm 133, one of the "songs of ascent," a text made up of only about thirty Hebrew words, a hymn to the joy of being a fraternal and united community, free from the worm of envy and the wound of hatred. The initial exclamation is sweet and fragrant: "Behold, how beautiful/good (*tôb*) and pleasant it is when brothers dwell together!" (v. 1). Saint Augustine took this hymn as the ideal motto of religious community life: "These words, this sweet voice, this soft melody, both in singing and in thought, has governed the monasteries . . . It has been the trumpet calling Christians to perfection. The whole universe has resounded with it and the dispersed have been reunited." The religious dimension of this fraternity is motivated by one of the two images used to celebrate it.

First of all, the image of the priestly balm of consecration is evoked: "It is like the precious oil poured upon the head, which runs down upon the beard, upon the beard of Aaron, which runs down on the collar of his robes" (v. 2). Balm also signifies hospitality (Ps 23:5) and of celebration and rejoicing (Ps 45:7), but is above all a reference to the ritual of priestly consecration (Ex 30:22–30), as the mention of Aaron, the father of the Levitical priesthood, suggests. Brotherhood is therefore a sacred reality that has within itself the very power of a consecration that pervades the whole personal being (in the East the beard is a symbol of vitality and vigorous virility). The Psalm could be, in the first place, an exhortation to the religious and priestly community, that it should be ready to recover unity and charity, by overcoming divisions, disputes, careerism, and jealousy.

The other comparison evokes the freshness of the dew that on the arid ground becomes a principle of renewal and fecundity. Isaiah even sings of it as the seed of the resurrection: "Thy dew is a dew of light, and they will bring shadow to the light" (Is 26:19). The Psalmist dreams poetically that the dew descends from the 9,200-foot peak of Mount Hermon, at the northern border of the Holy Land, and miraculously waters the whole land of Israel until it reaches the hot and distant hills of Jerusalem: "It is like the dew of Hermon, which falls on the mountains of Zion" (Ps 133:3, RSV). Brotherly love is a dew of freshness in the aridity and monotony of personal and community life; it must permeate the whole people of God, which only by being united in charity will receive the blessing, the spring of joyful life: "There the Lord has sent the blessing, life for evermore" (v. 3), the Psalmist concludes.

Nihil caritate dulcius, "nothing is sweeter than love," Saint Ambrose wrote in *De Officiis*. This is the *entolé megále*, "the greatest commandment, cardinal, principal" that Jesus wanted for the moral and spiritual commitment of the disciple (Mt 22:34–40, RSV). Christian *agápe*, sung in the famous Pauline hymn of the First Letter to the Corinthians (chapter 13), is accompanied in the New Testament by a parade of sister virtues like *philanthropía*, generous universal love; *philadelphía* for brothers and sisters in faith, "born anew, not of perishable seed but of imperishable, through the living and abiding word of God" (1 Pet 1:23, RSV); *koinonía*, which is the "communion" that is one of the four pillars of the Church of Jerusalem together with catechesis, prayer, and "the breaking of the bread" of the Eucharist (Acts 2:42, RSV); and *philoxenía*, hospitable reception of the stranger (Heb 13:1–2, RSV). We, however, would like to invoke now—in the wake of biblical numeric symbolism—the "numbers" that "measure" the authenticity of love of neighbor. We will entrust ourselves to four equations, beginning with the negative pole in the chromatic spectrum of love, that of hate.

The first equation, 7 to 77, is expressed in that terrible song of the sword intoned by Lamech, a descendant of Cain: "I have slain a man for wounding me, a young man for striking me. If Cain is avenged sevenfold, truly Lamech seventy-sevenfold" (Gn 4:23–24, RSV). It is the blind spiral of violence and war that shatters all social equilibrium and smears with blood the paths of history.

The second equation—7 to 70 x 7—correlates indirectly to the first, leading us to the exact opposite, where the formula of Lamech is reversed into the law of Christian forgiveness. It is in Jesus who, in response to Peter's suggestion of the 7 of fullness in forgiving—"Lord, how often shall my brother sin against me, and I forgive him? As many as seven times?"—proposed a number tending to infinity, transforming the equation of Lamech: "I do not say to you seven times, but seventy times seven" (Mt 18:21–22). An illustration of the equation is the parable of the two debtors who are compared on another numerical relationship, the 100 denarii and the 10,000 talents, to extol the infinite openness of the love that forgives (Mt 18:23–35, RSV).

With the third equation, 1 to 1, we return to a stage before love: distributive justice, expressed in the harsh form of the *lex talionis*. "Life for life, eye for eye, tooth for tooth, hand for hand, foot for foot, burn for burn, wound for wound, bruise for bruise" (Ex 21:23). It is the "what you hate, do not do to any one" (Tb 4:15, RSV), which Jesus would transform into the positive "whatever you wish that men would do to you, do so to them" (Mt 7:12, RSV). This positive sense is at the basis of another 1 to 1: "You shall love your neighbor as yourself" (Lev 19:18, RSV).

In this way let us proceed toward the surpassing of pure and simple justice, so as to introduce total and absolute love: it is the equation 3-4 to 1000. This already appears in a divine self-revelation at Sinai, "the biblical identity card of God," as it was called by Albert Gelin: "The Lord, the Lord, a God merciful and gracious, slow to anger, and abounding in steadfast love and faithfulness, keeping steadfast love for the thousandth generation, forgiving iniquity and transgression and sin. But does not let go without punishment, visiting the iniquity of the fathers upon the children and the children's children, to the third and the fourth generation" (Ex 34:6–7). In generational language intended to emphasize also the social aspect as well as the personal aspect of sin, it is known that divine justice that must have its truth and fullness, expressed through 3 and 4, which added together make 7. Nevertheless what dominates is the love that forgives because it does not know boundaries and is infinite, as indicated by the symbolic number 1000.

This love becomes universal, also embracing the foreigner, as required by the "code of the Testament" of Sinai: "You shall not wrong a stranger or oppress him, for you were strangers in the land of Egypt" (Ex 22:21, RSV). Additionally, the book of Leviticus would comment: "When a stranger sojourns with you in your land, you shall not do him wrong . . . rather you shall love him as one born among you; You will love him as yourself, for you were strangers in the land of Egypt" (Lev 19:33–34). Jesus deciphers and explicates the 1000 of the Old Testament in that extreme choice indicated for his disciples with the complete donation of themselves: "This is my commandment, that you love one another as I have loved you. Greater love has no man than this, that a man lay down his life for his friends" (Jn 15:12–13, RSV).

We cannot, however, leave the Psalter and its song of love without mentioning that antithetical presence, a genuine stumbling block, which are the "Psalms of imprecation," whose violence is so shocking as to have convinced the liturgy born from Vatican Council II to censor them, at least in official Christian prayer. In effect, they are a thorn in the side of Psalmic spirituality. The cascade of imprecations and of scalding symbols in Psalm 58 leaves one disconcerted: venom of a deaf serpent, fangs of lions, slime of a snail, the untimely birth of a woman, fire and thorns converge on the enemies of the worshiper and explode in incandescent flames: "O God, break the teeth in their mouths . . . Let the righteous rejoice when he sees the vengeance and wash his feet in the blood of the ungodly" (vv. 6, 10).

Of course, one must discount this exaggeration by remembering the intensity of Semitic language, just as one cannot ignore the desperation of the victims in the powerful Psalm 137, the *Super flumina Babylonis* with that terrible finale that records a tragic practice of war: "O daughter of Babylon, you devastator! Happy shall he be who requites you with what you have done to us! Happy shall he be who takes your little ones and dashes them against the rock!" (vv. 8–9, RSV).

Without resorting to the allegorical interpretations that soften these sinister humors of vengeance by dissolving them in metaphors of the battle against evil and Satan, one must recognize that in these, as in many other pages of the Bible, we feel the pulse of the historicity of Revelation: the Word of God is incarnated by adapting itself to human limitations and weakness in order to lead humanity—precisely through the progression of salvation history—toward a very different destination that can already be glimpsed in the Old Testament, before arriving at the fullness of the message of Christ. One reads, for example, in the book of Wisdom: "thou art merciful to all, for thou canst do all things, and overlook men's sins, waiting that they repent. For thou lovest all things that exist, and hast loathing for none of the things which thou hast made, for thou wouldst not have made anything if thou hadst hated it" (Wis 11:22–23).

In the finale of the terrible Psalm 58, judgment is left in the hands of God: "Surely there is a God who judges on earth" (v. 11, RSV). Behind the bloodied veil of the deprecatory words there is concealed, nonetheless, albeit in emphatic and exaggerated form, a particular virtue: disdain, which is very different from anger, which is instead a capital vice. It means unhesitatingly siding with good and justice and against evil, injustice, and depression, which not rarely in the Bible are personified as "enemies" or "the enemy." Let us not forget that Christ as well takes up the whip against the merchants and with the "Woes"—which are curses—against hypocrisy and injustice invites us not to reduce our moral proclamation and commitment to a pallid diplomatic appeal (Mt 23:13–36; Lk 6:24–26). "Our Lord," Bernanos affirmed, "did not write that we were the honey of the earth, but the salt. Now salt on living flesh is something that burns, but it also prevents rotting . . . The word of God is a burning fire; those who teach it cannot help but scorch their hands."

We have reached the end of our essential pilgrimage along the paths indicated by the Psalms. We have concluded with the song of fraternal love that is an invitation not to give into the temptation of rejection or fear of the other. As an Eastern parable says, seen from afar along the path of the desert of life, the other can seem confusedly like a beast, while from closer he may be mistaken for an aggressor. But when he is in front of you and you are looking him in the face, eye to eye, then comes the discovery: he is a brother you have not seen for years. At times we have evoked the Jordan as a symbol of our spiritual journey. Now we have come to our last approach of it. A Jewish aphorism tells us that "the Holy Land is marked by two lakes. The first is that of Tiberias, which receives water from the Jordan and gives it back. The second, instead, only receives, it accumulates and gives nothing. This is why it is called the Dead Sea!"

CHAPTER XVII

THE SEVEN STARS OF THE WORD

Lectio Divina

It is surprising, but the affirmation that we will now cite belongs to the thinker who has fought the most for the abandonment of Judeo-Christian culture, to such an extent that he entitled one of his works *Antichrist.* Now, in the preparatory material for his work *The Dawn* (1881) the philosopher Friedrich Nietzsche wrote: "Between what we feel in reading the Psalms and what we feel in reading Pindar or Petrarch there is the same difference as between one's own country and a foreign land." The Bible, above all in the Protestant formation of this author—in particular the Psalms that were sung in worship—constituted the familiar horizon, the ear remained full of its echoes as the conch preserves the sound of the sea, even when it is far away. At the conclusion of our journey in the world of prayer, where the divine Word and the human intersect, let us propose a guide for the spiritual reading of the Psalter and of every page of the Bible.

Tradition, especially the monastic tradition of the Middle Ages, developed the fundamental canons for this *lectio divina*, in different articulations but substantially anchored to the four movements of *lectio*, which leads to the full "reading" of the biblical text selected, of the *meditatio*, in which there is discovered in profundity the meaning of Scripture and the divine voice that speaks to us, which is the prayerful and contemplative response of the human voice to the Lord who has spoken, and finally of *actio*, which transforms into a choice of life the word that has been listened to, meditated and prayed upon. Let us, instead, entrust ourselves now to the Bible itself, which suggests to us directly how to read it in spiritual fullness. We discover this kind of method in a historical book that at first sight is a bit arid, Nehemiah, the "secular" guide along with Ezra the priest in the rebirth of the Jewish state after the trauma of the Babylonian exile. In front of us is chapter eight, which we will examine only in its essential parts.

We are perhaps in 444 B.C., on the first day of the seventh month of Tishrei, which inaugurated the new year. It is an autumn afternoon, and the whole community is gathered together in the courtyard in front of the Water Gate, at the southeast of the temple of Zion. Men, women, and even children, "all who could hear with understanding," converge on this space, where in the middle of a stage stands Ezra, surrounded by the religious authorities. In his hand he holds the scroll of the Torah, the Law, probably an initial version of the current Pentateuch. It is a solemn commentary that turns into a sort of spiritual retreat "from early morning until midday." The assembly is on its feet and the ritual opens with a priestly blessing. From here on we would like to emphasize seven elements that constitute a constellation of acts to be performed for a full and effective hearing of the Word of God.

These are distributed along two movements. The first is of an intellectual nature, it is a work of exegesis, an "extraction of" (*ek-heghéomai*) its literal and spiritual meaning, grasping its message without overlapping any other ideas, so as to avoid an "eisegesis" of the text, which is a "bringing to" (*eis-heghéomai*) one's own convictions. Verse eight is, in this regard, fundamental because it combines the three "exegetical" acts, destined for the comprehension of the biblical page. One begins with "reading the book of the Law of God in distinct sections." In the Jewish tradition the Bible is called *miqra'*, "reading, proclamation" (the same root as the word "Qur'an"). This is such a significant act that it gave rise in Christianity to the ministry of Lector, a task that should be exercised with competence and refinement, in part because it is the first unveiling of the Word. Silent reading is recent in the history of culture and is tied to Renaissance humanism, so much so that biblical "meditation" (*hgh*) is literally a "murmuring" of the lips.

The "distinct sections" are, according to the Hebrew term used (*prsh*), the "pericopes" (*parashijjôt*), the portions of text that constitute the liturgical lectionary. Some also assign this term the value of "translation," given that Aramaic was spoken at the time; afterward the *targum*, the Aramaic paraphrase of the Hebrew sacred text, would be a constant practice. That of the versions remains another delicate and decisive chapter for the proclamation of the Bible, given that every version—as the great Cervantes said—is like turning over a tapestry with its threads elongated and the scenes inverted, less clear and colorful. There is always a distance with respect to the original, a distance that must be bridged through explanation and commentary.

The second element is precisely the "explanation of the meaning." In Hebrew this is a sapiential expression that permits one to cross the barrier of mere literalism, which can lead to the precipice of fundamentalism. There is therefore a need for the wise commentary that can open the secrets of Scripture in its literal meanings, a commentary that is complete and spiritual-moral. A famous rabbinical saying has it that "every word of the Torah has seventy faces," or every sacred word is like a rock broken by the hammer that emits a thousand sparks. One reads in Psalm 62:12: "God has said one word, two have I heard." This is the work of hermeneutics, meaning of the correct criteria of interpretation of a text that, as Benedict XVI repeatedly affirmed both in *Verbum Domini* and in the concrete exercise of his triptych of books on Jesus Christ, demands the respect of the two dimensions of Scripture.

Just as the Word is divine, eternal, transcendent, but is also historical and contingent "flesh," so also the Word of God requires, on the one hand, that it be kept intact in its divine quality, but also, on the other hand, that it be respected in its incarnation in historical human words.

It demands, that is, both a theological and a historical-critical interpretation without opposition and without simplifications, but rather in constant integration. So it is important—as the philosopher Emmanuel Lévinas suggested—"to go beyond the verse" without ignoring it, which means situating it in the broader fabric (*textus*) of the whole Canon of the sacred Scriptures, of the unity of Revelation.

The third and last phase of this first movement is its final fruit: "understanding the reading." In this case as well, a sapiential word is used: the verb *bîn*, which evokes an intellectual understanding but also "*une connaissance savoureuse*," flavorful and truly sapiential, to use an expression of the philosopher Jacques Maritain. True biblical "knowing" involves the aspects of intellect, will, emotion, and action, thus becoming a "symbolic" or comprehensive experience, which culminates in loving knowledge. To read, to explain, to understand are therefore the first three stars that are kindled in the sky of the acceptance of the Word of God. As an aside let us note that the Jewish tradition also added the act of "writing" a copy of the Torah, an operation now carried out by scribes with brilliant black ink on gleaming white parchment, so that the Word may shine, and to be written with a vegetable or animal quill, and not with metal, because metal is used for weapons.

There now opens before us the second movement, which includes four acts of an existential nature. In chapter eight of Nehemiah it is noted for the first time that "the ears of all the people were attentive to the book of the law" (v. 3, RSV) and that "they heard the words of the law" (v. 9, RSV). The first interior action is therefore "listening," which is much more than mere "hearing": it is the verb of obedient and joyful adherence. It is significant that the constant admonition of Deuteronomy is the Shemaʿ Jisraʾel, "Hear, O Israel!" an appeal that leads to the profession of faith: "The Lord our God is one Lord" (Dt 6:4, RSV). If the ear is open, or rather "dug out," as it literally says in Psalm 40:7, calling to mind the pierced ear of the obedient servant, the heart is so swept away as to generate tears of repentance for the evil committed.

The second vital act is visible in the eyes of the believer who weeps over his faults, so much so that Ezra must exhort those present: "'Do not mourn or weep.' For all the people wept when they heard the words of the law" (Neh 8:9, RSV).

From conversion is unleashed the act of love that moves the hands in acts of charity. This is the third movement of adherence to the Word of God. The priest invites the assembly to "send portions [of rich meat and sweet wine] to him for whom nothing is prepared" (v. 10, RSV), and the people immediately begin to "send portions and to make great rejoicing, because they had understood the words that were declared to them" (v. 12, RSV). One thus has the realization of the constant prophetic proclamation: "I desire steadfast love and not sacrifice" (Hos 6:6, RSV), an appeal that—as we know—only dialectically rejected worship, while in reality it was demanding that this be combined with practical effort for justice.

Immediately afterward comes the fourth and last element, celebration, "for this day is consecrated to our Lord" (v. 10). This liturgy is solemnly described afterward in the part of the text that speaks of the feast of Booths, the commemoration of the sojourn of Israel in tents during the march to the Promised Land: "Go out to the hills and bring branches of olive, wild olive, myrtle, branches of palm, and other leafy trees to make booths, as it is written" in the book of the Law (v. 15).

So let us make shine these seven stars that illuminate the journey of *lectio divina*, a "sweet battle with the Word of God, a battle more joyful than any peace," as the medieval author Rupert of Deutz says: to read, to explain, to understand, to listen, to convert, to act, to celebrate. The first movement involves the mind and rationality, understanding and comprehension, while in the second ears, eyes, hands, celebration unite in recognizing, as Vatican II teaches, that "the word of God is so great that it stands as the support and energy of the Church, the strength of faith for her sons, the food of the soul, the pure and everlasting source of spiritual life" (*Dei Verbum*, no. 21). We have also been led to this by this "wonderful treasury of prayers" (*Dei Verbum*, no. 15) that make up the Psalter, the *Tehillîm*, the "praises" that rise to God in the luminous days of joy as festive hymns and in those of the darkness of suffering as imploring supplications.

Through the *ars orandi*, which means praying in a beautiful and just way, it is possible to learn the *ars credendi*, or an authentic and profound faith. In Psalmic prayer and in its whole variegated thematic, literary, and spiritual rainbow one encounters the theophany, the God who reveals himself in the primacy of *charis-caritas*, grace-love, as Creator of the universe, as Lord in the temple and in the liturgy, as the God of history, and also manifests himself in his Messiah and in the man and woman who are his "image." Prayer thus becomes "theology," the discourse of God and about God. But in Psalmic prayer is also revealed our face. There is therefore an anthropology that traces the many lineaments of our human reality.

We have thus encountered faith upheld by trust, creatural limitation, sick and suffering man, man the sinner, man without God, man the wise, the priest, death and the afterlife, family and society, fraternal love. Precisely for this reason we can repeat in an ecumenical spirit the appeal that Luther in his *Preface to the Psalter* (1531) addressed to Christians that they might have "such a familiarity with the Psalms as to know them by memory," aware that they are in full accord with the Our Father: "The Psalter serves to understand the Our Father and both of them make an identical sound." And he concluded: "Those who have begun to pray with the Psalms in a serious and regular way will soon abandon the other easy, particular pious prayers and will say: 'Certainly there is not in these the power, the vigor, the fire that I find in these!'"

But for a more profound and full hearing of the Word of God it is necessary to create a halo of "white" silence, which is not a mere absence of songs, as happens in "black" silence, gloomy and nightmarish. Rather, it is a silence that hosts within itself a message, as happened to the prophet Elijah on Sinai when the epiphany of God did not appear in the "great and strong wind [that] rent the mountains, and broke in pieces the rocks," nor in an earthquake and not even in the fire. God had revealed himself with the mysterious word of silence, *qôl demamah daqqah*, the "still small voice," also similar to the "whispering of a light breeze," as one can also translate these three Hebrew words (1 Kg 19:11–12). The name of God, as the Jewish tradition would teach, is made up of four unpronounceable consonants, and yet it is a personal name that reveals itself, works, and saves.

Let us seek, then, to envelop our liturgical and personal reading of the Bible more often in the aureola of silence, as suggested by Dietrich Bonhoeffer, a Christian witness we have already referred to, a victim of Nazi inhumanity that denies God: "Let us make silence before listening to the Word of God, so that our thoughts may already be directed to the word. Let us make silence after listening to the Word of God, so that it may still talk to us, live and dwell in us. Let us make silence early in the morning so that God may have the first word. Let us make silence before going to bed, so that the last word may belong to God. Let us make silence solely for love of the Word."

SAINT BENEDICT + PRESS

Saint Benedict Press publishes books, Bibles, and multimedia that explore and defend the Catholic intellectual tradition. Our mission is to present the truths of the Catholic faith in an attractive and accessible manner.

Founded in 2006, our name pays homage to the guiding influence of the Rule of Saint Benedict and the Benedictine monks of Belmont Abbey, just a short distance from our headquarters in Charlotte, NC.

Saint Benedict Press publishes under several imprints. Our TAN Books imprint (TANBooks.com), publishes over 500 titles in theology, spirituality, devotions, Church doctrine, history, and the Lives of the Saints. Our Catholic Courses imprint (CatholicCourses.com) publishes audio and video lectures from the world's best professors in Theology, Philosophy, Scripture, Literature and more.

For a free catalog, visit us online at
SaintBenedictPress.com

Or call us toll-free at
(800) 437-5876